Pickwick

A Musical based on Charles Dickens's
Posthumous Papers of the Pickwick Club

Book by Wolf Mankowitz
Lyrics by Leslie Bricusse
Music by Cyril Ornadel

Samuel French - London
New York - Toronto - Hollywood

ISBN 0 573 08085 2

Please see page vii for further copyright information.

Reproduced and printed by Halstan & Co. Ltd., Amersham, Bucks., England

PICKWICK

Originally presented at the Saville Theatre, London, by
Bernard Delfont and Tom Arnold, in July 1963 with the
following cast:

Hot Drinks Seller	Norman Warwick
Cold Drinks Seller	Ian Burford
Turnkey	Brendan Barry
Pickwick	Harry Secombe
Augustus Snodgrass	Julian Orchard
Tracy Tupman	Gerald James
Nathaniel Winkle	Oscar Quitak
Roker	Reg Grey
Tony Weller	Robin Wentworth
Sam Weller	Teddy Green
Mr Wardle	Michael Logan
Rachel	Hilda Braid
Isabella	Vivienne St George
Emily	Jane Sconce
Fat Boy	Christopher Wray
Mr Jingle	Anton Rodgers
Mary	Dilys Watling
Mrs Bardell	Jessie Evans
Dr Slammer	Brendan Barry
Bardell Jnr	Terry Collins
1st Officer	Roger Ostime
2nd Officer	Norman Warwick
Skaters	Donald Graham & Joan Ismay
Landlord	Brian Casey
Dodson	Michael Darbyshire
Fogg	Tony Sympson
Judge	Colin Cunningham
Usher	David Harris
Sgt Snubbins	Brendan Barry
Sgt Buzfuz	Peter Bull

**Passers-by, Ostlers, Debtors, Maids, Drinkers and Pot
Boys:**

Roy Evans, Barrie Irwin, Jonnie Christen, Donald
Graham, Roger Ostime, Norman Warwick, Colin
Cunningham, Reg Grey, Ian Burford, David Harris,

Brian Casey, Brendan Barry, Dave Armour, Alan Mack, Harold Brookstone, Peter Wilson, Paul Silber, John Bohea, Richard Keene

Honor Lewis, Suzanne Kerchiss, Anna Leroy, Carol Naylor, Judy Nash, Jean Ann Page, Vivienne Ross, Rita McKerrow, Helena Leahy, Beryl Hall, Pamela Beesley, Joan Ismay, Joy Measures

Directed by **Peter Coe**
Designed by **Sean Kenny**

ACT I

ACT II

The action takes place in and around London and Rochester in the year 1827

MUSICAL NUMBERS

ACT I

1	**Overture**	–	
2	**Business is Booming**	–	Hot Drinks Seller, Cold Drinks Seller, Turnkey, Hot Potato Man, Bird Seller
3	**Debtors' Lament**	–	The Company
3A	**Talk**	–	Sam Weller and the Company
4	**That's What I'd Like For Christmas**	–	Pickwick and the Company
5	**The Pickwickians**	–	Pickwick, Snodgrass, Tupman and Winkle
5A	**The Pickwickians** (*reprise*)	–	Pickwick, Snodgrass, Tupman and Winkle
6	**A Bit Of A Character**	–	Jingle, Snodgrass, Winkle and Tupman
6A	**Quadrille**	–	Orchestra
7	**There's Something About You**	–	Jingle, Rachel and Company
8	**Learn A Little Something**	–	Sam Weller and Mary
9	**You've Never Met A Feller Like Me**	–	Pickwick and Sam Weller
10	**Look Into Your Heart**	–	Pickwick and Mrs Bardell
	or		
10	**I'll Never Be Lonely Again**	–	Pickwick and Mrs Bardell
10A	**Talk** (*reprise*)	–	Sam Weller
10B	**The Duel**	–	
11	**Winter Waltz**	–	The Company
11A	**Winter Waltz** (*ending*)	–	Orchestra
11B	**Entr'Acte**	–	

ACT II

12	**A Hell Of An Election**	–	The Company
13	**Very**	–	Jingle
13A	**A Hell Of An Election** (*reprise*)	–	Orchestra
14	**If I Ruled The World**	–	Pickwick and the Company
15	**The Trouble With Women**	–	Sam Weller and Tony Weller

vi

COPYRIGHT INFORMATION

(See also page ii)

This play is fully protected under the Copyright Laws of the British Commonwealth of Nations, the United States of America and all countries of the Berne and Universal Copyright Conventions.

All rights, including Stage, Motion Picture, Radio, Television, Public Reading, and Translation into Foreign Languages, are strictly reserved.

No part of this publication may lawfully be reproduced in ANY form or by any means—photocopying, typescript, recording (including video-recording), manuscript, electronic, mechanical, or otherwise—or be transmitted or stored in a retrieval system, without prior permission.

Licences for amateur performances are issued subject to the understanding that it shall be made clear in all advertising that the audience will witness an amateur performance; that the names of the authors of the plays shall be included on all announcements and on all programmes; and that the integrity of the authors' work will be preserved.

The Royalty Fee is subject to contract and subject to variation at the sole discretion of Samuel French Ltd.

In Theatres or Halls seating Six Hundred or more the fee will be subject to negotiation.

In Territories Overseas the fee quoted in this Acting Edition may not apply. A fee will be quoted on application to our local authorized agent, or if there is no such agent, on application to Samuel French Ltd, London.

VIDEO RECORDING OF AMATEUR PRODUCTIONS

Please note that the copyright laws governing video-recording are extremely complex and that it should not be assumed that any play may be video-recorded *for whatever purpose* without first obtaining the permission of the appropriate agents. The fact that a play is published by Samuel French Ltd does not indicate that video rights are available or that Samuel French Ltd controls such rights.

INTRODUCTION

The original production of *Pickwick* was designed by Sean Kenny and the staging of it was a natural extension of our work together on two other British musicals—*Lock Up Your Daughters* and *Oliver!* On the whole colours were muted—the set was in solid wood, heavy in construction and dark brown in colour, the costumes basically the same earthy colours, with brighter touches for certain of the characters.

One of the basic principles of the staging of all three shows was that, before putting any set on the stage, as much space should be created as possible. The flies were stripped of everything not belonging to the production including all cloths, battens, masking blacks, everything. The lamps were allowed to hang in full view of the audience, so that space and light were seen between them and beyond them. The brick back wall of the theatre was painted in abstract multicolours, so that when different coloured light was thrown on it, it changed for each scene. The wings were also stripped of all the usual masking clutter and the front curtain was taken up as far as it would go regardless of what it exposed.

In this way even the smallest of stages is made to look vast, and the mobility of scenery and action is altogether easier and more fluid. There is also, in my mind, a degree of honesty in doing this. The idea that you cover everything you don't want the audience to see in black cloth has always seemed odd to me. The audience sees bits of black cloth everywhere and tries to figure out what could be underneath. If such an idea were extended to the home it becomes apparent how silly it can be. If one were to throw a piece of black cloth over an unwanted radiator, it would only bring attention to the radiator. Much better to have the radiator removed or to make a feature of it. I have the same attitude to black-outs between scenes in the theatre. The black-out is supposed to make it impossible for the audience to see what is going on on stage. But in fact because light is always leaking from somewhere in a theatre, the audience can normally see everything and sitting in front of one of these so called black-outs one is reminded of Frankie Howerd's choice observation that stage hands "should be heard but not seen".

Adopting the principle that black-outs only make things more difficult for actors and stage staff, it means that all scene changing needs to be done in full view of the audience. In *Pickwick* the changes were done by the actors in their costumes and were executed to exact bars of music. They played a part in the musical structure of the piece as much as everything else. In fact with this particular show we went even further with the principle, and on two occasions the company changed their costumes in front of the audience. This occurred at the beginning and end of the flashback, and served to indicate that the company was going to tell the story within the flashback and, of course, play all the parts therein by the simple means of costume change.

The London set consisted of five wooden towers with various platforms and stairways on them, each tower a different size and shape. They were placed on castors so that they could swivel a hundred and eighty degrees, travel anywhere on stage, and fit together at will like children's blocks to make rooms or streets or prisons as needed. Immediately they were in position for any particular scene, flying pieces came in to augment and decorate what was already there. It took four or five men to operate each tower and to brake it in position. These men were expected to sing as they worked.

It may not be possible on smaller stages and with less finance and time available to rehearse these complicated changes, or to use such massive scenery. However if the principle of staging is acceptable it should be possible to construct lighter pieces to function in the same way and be manipulated by the actors. If the designer keeps in mind the idea of children's blocks that fit together in various ways, the degree of complication of each block is entirely up to him and the director, as is indeed the actual size and material of the block. If flying is at all possible, the mobile pieces could be skeletal, leaving what is flown to provide the body of the scenery. If the pieces placed by the actors were thought of as frames to surround and embellish what was flown in, the problem of setting and striking would be a simple one.

A word about the ice-skating scene. It is my fault that the scene is there at all but it seemed too big an opportunity for fun and spectacle to leave out. However, keeping ice frozen in the theatre is a day and night occupation and not a guaranteed success anyway. It should be possible to dress roller skates to make them represent ice skates.

There should in any case be a lot of representation in the show. An example is the use of life-size horses made of wire—horses that can be seen through— used for the stage coach and led in by ostlers. The audience got more fun out of that idea than they would have derived from the appearance of a couple of cart horses. They will react in the same way when they see your Pickwickians ice-skating on thinly disguised roller skates. Two children were used for the exhibition skating, which gave it charm. Pickwick's fall through the ice was done by using the trap and putting over it a piece of thin white polystyrene. This looks like ice and breaks easily under weight.

Lastly it must be remembered that the best inspiration for actors, director and designer, is the *Pickwick Papers* itself and the remarkable drawings that went with the original editions. All our costume designs, groupings and activities of the small parts played by the crowd in the debtors' prison and the election scene, was taken from the appropriate chapters in the novel. The sections of the book which are dramatised in this show are required re-reading for everyone concerned.

Peter Coe

PICKWICK

Music 1. Overture

ACT I

SCENE 1

Outside the Fleet Prison gates

When the CURTAIN rises the stage is empty of actors and scenery. The opening street cries are heard off stage. The traders come in wheeling their carts and singing. Customers and passers-by accumulate slowly making the scene busier and busier. It is a cold night. Everyone stamps about, blowing on their hands

Music 2: Song: Business Is Booming   music

Hot Drinks Seller Business is booming!
Cold Drinks Seller Business is blooming slow!
Hot   Takings are zooming!
Cold   Takings are blooming low!

                     I must be mad selling cold drinks!
Hot   My drinks are piping hot!
                     Precious-as-gold drinks—
Bird Seller (*shouting*) Birds and bird cages!
Cold   Freezing cold drinks are not!
Hot Potato Man (*shouting*) Hot potatoes!
Cold   Not in the winter!
Hot   No, but in June!
Cold   But this is mid-winter!
Hot   But June will be here soon!
Cold   Please make it soon!
                     Flaming June!
Bird Seller (*shouting*) Birds and bird cages

Hot   Business this week's twice as good as last week!
Cold   Business last week worse than what it's been this past
                     week!

Hot	Cheer up, Charley, next week may become a fast week— a vast week!
Cold	One more week like this week, next week is me last week!

Hot	Hot whisky toddy!
Hot Potato Man (*shouting*)	Hot potatoes!
Bird Seller (*shouting*)	Birds and bird cages!
Cold	Cold lemonade and lime!
Bird Seller (*shouting*)	Birds and bird cages!
Hot	Warms up your body— Only a penny a time!
Hot Potato Man (*shouting*)	Hot potatoes!
Cold	Only a matter of time!

The prison gate flies in. This is the only piece of scenery

The Turnkey emerges from the prison carrying a huge ring of keys, yawns and stretches his arms

Hot (*speaking*) Morning, Mr Turnkey, sir; and 'ow's things in the Fleet 'otel today?

The Turnkey grins

Turnkey (*singing*)	Business is booming— Prison is forever full! Free board and rooming—
Cold	Not a bad trick to pull!

Turnkey	My clients mainly are debtors— That is their lucky lot! Can't pay their betters— So they come here to rot!
Cold	Not very pleasant!
Hot	Life can be cruel!
Turnkey	It's not that unpleasant— Each day we give them gruel! (*To Cold*) Piping hot gruel!
Cold	(*licking his lips*) Steaming gruel!
Turnkey	Pray don't think the Fleet is full of flops and floozies!— We've got someone coming here because he chooses!
All (*amazed*)	*Chooses?*
Turnkey	Widder sued him—breach of promise—she accuses—he loses— Bigwig name of Pickwick, *can* pay but refuses!

Pickwick enters on top of a wheelbarrow containing his luggage, pushed by Sam Weller. If this presents difficulties he can march on followed by Sam carrying the luggage. There is an orchestral accompaniment to his entrance.

Once the Turnkey has locked the gate it flies out slowly. The Turnkey sings his last lines—the traders call their cries as they go out

Turnkey	Business is booming!
Hot	Hot whisky toddy!
Hot Potato Man	Hot potatoes!
Bird Seller	Birds and bird cages!
Cold	Cold as a shiver!
Hot Potato Man	Hot potatoes!
Bird Seller	Birds and bird cages!
Turnkey	Prisons for ever full!
Hot	Keeps out the cold and grime!
Hot Potato Man	Hot potatoes!
Bird Seller	Birds and bird cages!
Cold	Cold lemonade and lime!
Turnkey	Business is booming!
Hot	Hot whisky toddy!
Hot Potato Man	Hot potatoes!
Bird Seller	Birds and bird cages!
Cold	Good for your liver!
Turnkey	Business is booming!
Hot	Warms up your body!
Turnkey	Business is booming!
Hot	Hot whisky toddy!
Cold	Good for your liver!

The last of the traders has gone

SCENE 2

Interior of the Fleet Prison

The Debtors enter singing and pushing their prison into position. The women bring whatever properties are needed and also provide a chorus of coins clanging in metal mugs. The change is done in fairly subdued lighting. It is complete by the end of the lament. This is the first change that the actors operate and the work motive suits the prison scene well

Music 3. Song: The Debtors' Lament   music

Chorus	Help the poor debtors!
	Help the poor debtors!
	Help the poor debtors to live!
	Each little ha'penny you give
	Helps the poor debtors to live!
	Each little ha'penny you give
	Helps the poor debtors, helps the poor debtors—

Helps the poor debtors, helps the poor debtors.

The Lights come up on Pickwick and reveal his growing horror at the place—a galleried building guarded by Roker and the Turnkey. At different levels of the galleries and around him in the courtyard are the debtors; they include complete families from old people to children who argue, shout, play games, read, etc.

Pickwick You don't mean to tell me that all those poor people *live* down these wretched dungeons?

Roker All debtors, sir, all hopelessly in debt, sir.

Turnkey All of 'em.

Pickwick But *live* down *there*!

Roker Yes, sir, live down there.

Turnkey Yes, sir, and die down there too very often.

Roker What of that?

Turnkey Who's going to say anything agin it?

Roker Good enough in all conscience for debtors. Very grateful they should be free as they are to have their loved ones with them. I maintain, sir, that a man who will not pay his debts to society, owns no comfort that society can offer. Unless he can pay, of course. Come sir, let me give you the conducted tour.

Turnkey This 'ere is what we call the Coffee Room flight.

Roker And the one above is somewhat amusingly dubbed the Painted Room.

Turnkey That's because a lot of them as has spent a good many years here have done it over with their initials and paintings and that.

Roker Where we are now, sir, we call the Fair. Yes, I daresay there is room for a little one there. Move them over.

Turnkey (*shouting*) New chum coming up.

There is a commotion at the gate. Sam and Tony Weller arrive loaded with Pickwick's bags and various comforts

Sam (*thoughtfully*) Now look here, old codger, this here is a prison for them what don't pay their debts, correct?

Tony Correct.

Sam In which case, anybody who didn't pay his debt would have the right to stay here, correct?

Tony Correct.

Sam Lend me ten sovereigns.

Tony You mean my life savings?

Sam Correct.

Tony gropes under his greatcoat and heaves out a large leather purse. Grunts, grumbles and noises of objections from the crowded cell

(*Shouting*) Don't you agree to nothing, sir! (*He runs up to Pickwick*)

Debtor (*to Roker*) You're not putting that poor fellow down here, are you?

Roker Mind your business, sir. Pay your debts, sir, then you will have the right to speak, sir.

Sam runs over to Roker and the Turnkey

Sam Where are you putting my gentleman?

Roker In here.

Sam What about this, then? (*He flashes the money*)

The Turnkey holds out his hand. Sam slips him some coins

What can you do for us in the way of a nice room?

Turnkey I got the perfect room over here.

Sam Here hold on, dad. (*To Tony*) Do I or do I not owe you ten sov'reigns?

Tony You do.

Sam Will I or will I not pay my debt?

Tony You will not.

Sam You're not going to have me bunged in the nick for it?

Tony I will. I stand on my rights.

Sam (*to the Turnkey*) Lead on, ossifer. A nice room for two.

Pickwick But Sam—I cannot allow you to do this.

Sam There's nothing you can do about it, sir. Every Englishman has the right not to pay his debts.

Roker exits

Tony has engaged the attention of the Turnkey and is apparently doing some sort of business with him

Turnkey Here's a room, young man.

Sam Yes, I see it.

Turnkey You wouldn't get a better room in the Farrington Hotel, would you?

Pickwick (*with an effort*) Well Sam, it seems to me that imprisonment for debt isn't all that bad.

Sam Sir, for a gentleman in your estate it's downright ridiculous.

Pickwick Sam, Sam, it's a matter of principle.

Sam Principle be damned. You are incarcerating yourself in this 'ere dungeon, for life, for what? For nothing, sir, other than that damnable principle. It's a crying shame. You've got to learn to talk your way out of things.

During the song Sam illustrates the incidents with the help of the Debtors who readily understand the moral of the chorus. Sam must be able to dance, and should use the ability in all his numbers

music   **Music 3A. Song: Talk**

Sam   If you're walking say down St Martin's Lane—
                   And you see a shilling sparkling in the rain—
                   Of course you'll pick it up—
                   For some poor blind beggar's cup—
                   But if the law should see you do it, then the
                       game is up!

                   You'll have to
                   Talk your way out of it!—
                   Talk your way out of it!
                   Talk around about a bit,
                   But talk!—

                   Or you'll be dead as mutton!

                   Talk your way out of it!—
                   Talk your way out of it!
                   Talk around about a bit,
                   But talk!

                   If you're stroll-ing, say, a-round So-ho Square
                   And you meet a dam-sel tak-ing in the air;
                   No doubt you'll ask her out
                   For a tin-y glass of gin;
                   Be sure that when you take her out, she does-n't
                       take you in.

                   You'll have to
                   Talk your way out of it.
                   Talk your way out of it.
                   Talk around about a bit.
                   But talk!

                   Or else she'll have you cornered!

                   Talk your way out of it.
                   Talk your way out of it.
                   Talk around about a bit.
                   But talk!

Sam and Chorus Talking wiv a toff—that's conversation!
                    Talking wiv a barmaid—that's chat!
                    Talking wiv a policeman—that's evidence!
                    One false move and that's that!

Sam   If you're stepping out in St. James's Park—

With some sweet young widder ready for a lark!
She asks you home to tea—
Then a knock comes at the door—
Her husband's very much alive and six foot
   three or four!

You'll have to
Sam and Chorus   Talk your way out of it!—
Talk your way out of it!
Talk around about a bit,
But talk!

Or he'll make mincemeat of you!

Talk your way out of it!—
Talk your way out of it!—
Talk around about a bit,
But talk!

Verse:

But conversation somehow isn't what it used to be!—
People say six words then start to get monotonous!
Thank the Lord that England still has raconteurs the
   likes of me—
Who can talk the hind legs off a hippopotamous!

From the ratters in the sewers
To the Guild of Master Brewers,
From the dustman to the noble Duke of York!
There is no one in this city—
From the Queen to this young pretty—
Not a soul to 'oom Sam Weller couldn't talk!

Resume half chorus

Sam and Chorus   Talking with a sport!—
That's entertainment!
Talking wiv a lawyer—
That's cash!
Talking wiv a bailiff—
That's suicide!
Out you go wiv a crash!

Sam   If you're standing say in Coventry Street—
And by chance you meet the law out on its beat—
And if the law should ask
Why aren't you home in bed—

	And why you reek of liquor and are standing on your	
	head!	
	You'll have to—	
Sam and Chorus	Talk your way out of it—	
	Talk your way out of it!—	
	Talk around about a bit,	
	But talk!	
Sam	Just say it's force of habit!	
	Talk your way out of it!—	
	Talk your way out of it!—	
	Talk around about a bit,	
	But talk!—	
	Or you'll get fourteen days, so—	
Sam and Chorus	Talk your way out of it!—	
	Talk your way out of it!—	
	Talk around about a bit,	
	But—	

Sam	Talk can get you out of trouble	**Chorus**	Talk!
	And into business and earn you double		Talk!
	Than what you got before you went		Talk!
	and took the trouble		Talk!
	To learn to talk		Talk!
	Talk your way out of it!		Talk!
	Learn to talk!		Talk!
	Talk your way out of it!		Talk!

(*Speaking*) Well, we must take what comes and learn from our experiences.

Pickwick I suppose you're right, Sam.

Sam We certainly 'ad plenty of them since we come together, sir, that first Christmas.

Pickwick What a Christmas that was, eh Sam?

Sam That's when I first met you, guvner, you and my Mary on the same Christmas—and two better presents a simple boot-black of genius never received. Christmas Eve, it was, guvner, Christmas Eve at the old *George and Vulture*.

This is the beginning of the flash-back. The Lights go down to a very low level with a spot remaining on Sam and Pickwick as they continue speaking. At the same time the Debtors rise and change into their "George and Vulture" costumes. Most of them are "under-dressed" and any extra clothes that are needed are hidden in their bundles of rags. All the discarded clothes are put into baskets and these are struck during the chorus

The scene is changed at the same time, the towers being moved to positions for the "George and Vulture" and flying pieces, if any, brought in. All is now ready for the action to commence after Pickwick sings "That's where it all began!"

Music 4. Song: That's What I'd Like For Christmas   music

Pickwick	Christmas Eve was the day we met, Sam!—
	That was the day I shan't forget!
	The *George and Vulture*—
Sam	That's right, sir!
Pickwick	It was Christmas Eve—
Sam	What a night, sir!
Pickwick	Christmas Eve at the *George and Vulture*!—
	That's where it all began, Sam—
	That's where it all began!

Scene 3

The Courtyard Of The George and Vulture, *a coaching station in South Rochester just before Christmas, 1827. Night*

We look into the greater rectangular galleried courtyard. Facing us, CS, as the gates which open out on to the street

Waiters and Pot Boys, together with Drinkers, Servants, Hawkers, Ostlers and Stablemen are bustling and hurrying

The Lights come up as the Chorus sing "Merry Christmas". All is ready at that moment and the transformation complete

Pickwick's table and chair are moved by ostlers during the chorus. The activity during the chorus is one of food and drink being unloaded from carts and passed into the inn either through doorways or by way of balconies, through windows. The servants handle the goodies with envy, since presumably they are for the guest and not for them

Pickwick	Turkeys bigger than I am—
	Snowflakes made of lace—
	That's what I'd like for Christmas!—
All	Merry Christmas!
Girls	Silk and satin from Siam—
	Soft upon my face.
	That's what I'd like for Christmas!—
	Merry Christmas!
Pickwick	Lots and lots of lovely presents ⸺ ⟩ CX IT
	For all my favourite friends! BACK
	Roasted goose and roasted pheasants—
	With cranberry an' very sad when it ends!

All	Boxes full of the best nuts— Chestnuts in the fire— That's my desire for Christmas—
Girls	Jingling bells and mingling smells Of toffee and coffee and caramels. Seasonal greetings but no farewells— That's what I'd like for Christmas!
All	Please permit me to wish you ENTER All that you wish me! That's what I'd like for Christmas!— Merry Christmas!
Girls **Men** **All**	All the kids singing carols— Barrels full of booze— That's what I'd choose for Christmas! All good cheer and gallons of beer— Drinking my fill till I'm full to here! Pleasantly plastered until New Year— That's what I'd like for Christmas!
Sam and Chorus	Lots and lots of lovely presents For all my favourite friends! Roasted goose and roasted pheasants— With cranberry an' very sad when it ends!
All	Boxes full of the best nuts— Chestnuts in the fire— That's my desire for Christmas!
Men	Every pretty poppet I know Kissing me under the mistletoe! Once they are there they just can't say "No"!
All	That's what I'd like this Christmastime— To hear every churchbell gaily chime—
Pickwick	Peace and goodwill, all the world's in rhyme!
All	That's what I'd like for Christmas!
Chorus	Ah!
Pickwick	Merry Christmas! Merry Christmas!
Chorus	Christmas!

The Pickwickians—Snodgrass, Tupman and Winkle—enter from the Inn at the end of Music 4

At that moment, a stage coach arrives, containing Mr Wardle, his two daughters Isabella and Emily and his sister Rachel. Also on the coach are Mr Jingle, a threadbare, vagrant, gentleman opportunist, shabbily dressed, and Joe the fat boy

Wardle (*alighting*) Pickwick!
Pickwick Wardle!

Isabella, Emily and Rachel start getting out of the coach

Wardle And how are you, sir? Well, I'm glad you're well, very glad I am
to be sure. Joe, Joe! Damn that boy, he's gone to sleep again. Be good
enough to pinch him, sir—in the leg if you please, nothing else wakes
him. Thank you. Undo the luggage, Joe. My daughters, Mr Pickwick—
my gals these are: Emily and Isabella, and that's my sister Miss Rachel
Wardle. She's a Miss, she is, and yet she ain't amiss: eh, sir, eh?

*Joe gets the luggage down and the Servants take it into the Inn. Jingle gets
down from the coach and, carrying a brown paper parcel, unobtrusively joins
the crowd. When Joe has finished moving the luggage he settles down on the
coach and falls asleep*

Rachel (*archly*) Oh you quiz!
Wardle I hope I'm not late for the Club Meeting?
Pickwick Not at all, sir. And may I introduce you, sir, and your daughters,
sir, to the other members of the Pickwick Club.

Music 5. Song: The Pickwickians   music

*This song has considerable impact if accompanied by some stylish choreo-
graphy. It should not be strenuous but it should indicate the essential refinement
and neatness of the archetypal Pickwickian*

Pickwick	Picture if you can A highly sensitive man— With the soul of a poet And with long flowing hair— A unique way of dressing that is—well—
Snodgrass	Debonair!
Pickwick	Debonair to say the least For the world is seldom graced With a gentleman as polished and refined as he— A man of culture and—
Snodgrass	Good taste!
Pickwick	Good taste! That's Snodgrass!
All	That's Snodgrass!

Beyond a shadow of a doubt, that's Snodgrass!

Pickwick   As delicate and gentle as a man can be—
Augustus Hilary Snodgrass—

Snodgrass   That's me!

Pickwick   Picture if you can
A most susceptible man—
Whose romantic emotions
Never seem to be spared—
But whose love of the ladies still remains—

Tupman   Unimpaired!

Pickwick   Unimpaired to say the least!
Give him just one tiny shove
And he'll fall with all the ardour of
a moonstruck youth—
Because he loves to be—

Tupman   In love!

Pickwick   In love! That's Tupman!

All   That's Tupman!
Beyond a shadow of a doubt, that's Tupman!

Pickwick   As near to passion's plaything as a man can be—
Tracy Pyramus Tupman—

Tupman   That's me!

Pickwick   Picture if you can
A most adventurous man—
With the heart of a lion
And the strength of a bear—
And a cool kind of courage that is—well—

Winkle   Very rare!

Pickwick   Very rare to say the least—
For it isn't every day
That you come upon a sportsman quite as fine as he—
The very essence of—

Winkle   Fair play!

Pickwick	Fair play! That's Winkle!
All	That's Winkle! Beyond a shadow of a doubt, that's Winkle!
Pickwick	As sporting and as dashing as a man can be— Nathaniel Herbert Winkle—

Winkle (*speaking*) That's me!

Wardle (*speaking*) And what about yourself, Pickwick?

Pickwick (*speaking*) Why bless my soul, I never thought about it!

Snodgrass	Picture if you can A shy intelligent man—
Tupman	Very few have an intellect As sparkling as his!
Winkle	Some may doubt that his genius is great—
All	But it is!
Snodgrass	Oh, it *is*, to say the least!
Tupman	And his praises we shall sing!
Winkle	We are proud to be acquainted with a great, great man!
Snodgrass	The man's a prince!
Tupman	A Duke!
Winkle	A King!
All	A King! That's Pickwick! That's Pickwick! Beyond a shadow of a doubt, that's Pickwick! As civilised and splendid as a man can be— Samuel Willoughby Pickwick—
Pickwick	That's me!
All	We are the satellites—
Pickwick	I am the hub!

All	Of that eminent society, the Pickwick Club! The Pickwick Club!

Emily, Isabella and Rachel, smitten by these glorious new-found heroes, gaze adoringly upon the unlikely objects of their ardour

Emily (*of Snodgrass*)	Picture if you can A shy, poetical man—
Isabella (*of Winkle*)	And a man full of courage, If he had half a chance—
Rachel (*of Tupman*)	And a man so romantic He is learning to dance.
Emily **Isabella** (*together*) **Rachel**	Special men, to say the least!— Of a type one seldom sees!
Emily	If a lady had a say In choosing whom she pleased.
Isabella	I'm pleased to say that we'd choose these!
Rachel	That's Tupman!—
Isabella	That's Winkle!—
Emily	Beyond a shadow of a doubt, That's Snodgrass!
Emily **Isabella** (*together*) **Rachel**	All three of them As flawless as the finest gem!—
Emily	Augustus!
Rachel	Tracy!
Isabella	Nathaniel!
Emily **Isabella** (*together*) **Rachel**	That's them!
Rachel	We're shy to tell them so—

Emily }		Aye, there's the rub!—

Emily
Isabella } (*together*)
Rachel

Aye, there's the rub!—
But we're mad about the members
Of the Pickwick Club!
The Pickwick Club!

Mrs Bardell and her son Georgie enter

The Chorus move into the Inn

Through her next speech Mrs Bardell bustles the party towards the entrance to the main parlour of the George and Vulture

Mrs Bardell Look at us standing about and you all frozen and famished. James! This way, ladies. (*Calling*) James! Get a nice steaming toddy ready for Mister Wardle. I trust that's your inclination, Mr Wardle, sir.
Wardle You know my taste, Mrs Bardell.
Mrs Bardell Mr Pickwick, sir, this way. Come along, Georgie.

Pickwick, Wardle, the Ladies and Mrs Bardell exit

Snodgrass, Winkle and Tupman catch the eyes of the three ladies as they go

Winkle (*reacting to Isabella*) Tally ho! Is that little vixen old Wardle's daughter?
Snodgrass (*reacting to Emily*) Those eyes! My God, Tupman, those limpid violet eyes. I am trapped, sir!
Tupman (*reacting to Rachel*) Devil take me, Snodgrass! What a bust!

Pickwick returns

Pickwick I heard that gentlemen. May I remind you once again, members of the Pickwick Club, just what our principles are!
Tupman Absolutely!
Winkle Of course!
Snodgrass Definitely!

Music 5A. Song: The Pickwickians (*reprise*)

All	Picture if you can
	This indestructible clan—
	Every man is determined—
	Every man is resolved—
	In affairs of the heart he will remain—
Pickwick	Uninvolved!
Tupman	Uninvolved to say the least—
Snodgrass	Unattached and fancy free!
Winkle	And if ever any of us should lose his head—

Pickwick	He's always got the other three!
All	That's friendship! That's friendship!
	Beyond a shadow of a doubt, that's friendship!
	We're never going to marry 'cos it's too much fuss!
	Four superior bachelors—
	That's us!
Winkle	That is the essence—
Snodgrass	The gist—
Tupman	And the nub—
All	Of the principles of freedom of the Pickwick Club!
	The Pickwick Club!

Pickwick exits

Jingle, who has been observing the group from a distance, moves up to them

Jingle Haven't had the pleasure, gentlemen. Alfred Jingle, gentleman of leisure, travelled down with the ladies there.
Tupman Indeed, indeed, sir.
Jingle Excellent Club, yours—much to my liking. Poet, sir?
Winkle My friend, Mr Snodgrass, has a strong poetic turn.
Snodgrass (*taking out a notebook*) I have a little poem here.
Jingle (*not looking at it*) So have I. Epic poem—ten thousand lines— revolution of July—composed it on the spot.
Snodgrass You mean you were actually present at that glorious scene?
Jingle I should just say I was. Mars by Day, Apollo by night—bang the field-piece, twang the lyre. Noble time, sir; noble time. (*To Winkle*) Sportsman, sir?
Winkle A little, sir.
Jingle Fine pursuit, sir—fine pursuit. Dogs, sir?
Winkle Not just now.
Jingle Ah! You should keep dogs—fine animals—sagacious creatures—dog of my own once—pointer—surprising instinct—out shooting one day— entering enclosure—whistled dog—dog stopped—whistled again—called him—"Ponto, Ponto"—dog wouldn't move—dog transfixed—staring at a board—looked up, saw an inscription—"Gamekeeper has orders to shoot all dogs found in this enclosure"—wouldn't pass it—wonderful dog—valuable dog, that—very! Friend of the ladies, are you, sir?
Tupman Not really, sir.
Jingle Isabella, Emily, Rachel. Fine girls, those, sir, fine girls—English girls not so fine as Spanish—noble creatures—jet hair—black eyes—lovely forms—sweet creatures—beautiful.
Tupman You have been in Spain, sir?
Jingle Lived there—ages.
Tupman Many conquests, sir?
Jingle Conquests! Thousands. Don Bolaro Fizzgig—Grand Duke—only daughter—Donna Christina—splendid creature—loved me to dis-

traction—jealous father—high-souled daughter, handsome Englishman—Donna Christina in despair—prussic acid—stomach pump in
my portmanteau—operation performed—old Bolaro in ecstasies—
consent to our union—join hands and floods of tears—romantic story—
very.

Tupman Is that lady in England now, sir?

Jingle Dead, sir—dead. Never recovered the stomach pump—undermined
constitution—fell a victim.

Snodgrass And her father?

Jingle Remorse and misery. Sudden disappearance—talk of the whole
city—search made everywhere—without success—public fountain in the
great square suddenly ceased playing—weeks elapsed—still a stoppage—
workmen employed to clean it—water drawn off—father-in-law discovered sticking head first in the main pipe, with a full confession in his
right boot—took him out, and the fountain played away again, as well
as ever.

Snodgrass Will you allow me to note that little romance down, sir? (*He
writes in his notebook*)

Jingle Certainly, sir, certainly—fifty more if you'd like to hear 'em. Take
my word for it, gentlemen, a little flair—courage—imagination—no battle
can't be won—simple matter—very!

Music 6. Song: A Bit Of A Character   music

I'm a bit of a character—
Quite a character!
Name of Alfred Jingle!
Twenty six and single—
More than willing to mingle.
All the ladies love me—
And strictly entre nous—
The ladies all admit
That I'm a bit of a character, too!

The Duchess of Dorking—
Famous for talking—
Promised if I wed her daughter,
Great big house—Virginia Water,
Ten thousand pounds!—
And a stupid but suitable spouse!
'Twas the talk of the town—
But I turned her down—
Cos I wasn't too keen on the house!

I'm a bit of a character—
Quite a character—
Name of Alfred Jingle!

Twenty six and single—
More than willing to mingle.

All the ladies love me—
From here to Timbuctoo—
The ladies all admit
That I'm a bit of a character, too!

Seville millionairess—
Born Buenos Aires—
Loved me with consuming passion!
Not unusual—quite the fashion!
Wanted to flee
From her husband, who's terribly nice!
Must have broken her heart
When we had to part—
But we couldn't agree on the price!

Pickwickians   He's a bit of a character—
Quite a character—
Name of Alfred Jingle!
Twenty six and single—
More than willing to mingle.

All the ladies love him
And send him billet-doux—
The ladies all admit
That's he's a bit of a character, too!

Jingle   Bavarian Contessa—
Raised in Odessa—
Wealthy mother stiff with roubles—
Saw in me a man with scroubles.
Daughter adored me—
I wasn't accepting a crumb!
They were visibly moved—
And the future proved
I was far better off with her mum!

Pickwickians   He's a bit of a character—
Quite a character—
Name of Alfred Jingle!
Twenty six and single—
More than willing to mingle.

All the ladies love him—
For he's their dream come true!
The ladies all admit

That's he's a bit of a character, too!

Jingle   Italian marquisa—
                    Owned half of Pisa—
                    Not marquisa, no—mar*chesa*!
                    Was it Pisa? Maybe Stresa!
                    Pure as a pearl,
                    But suspicious and jealous as jade!
                    I'd have been with her yet,
                    But she got upset
                    When she found me in bed with her maid!

Pickwickians   He's a bit of a character—
                    Quite a character—
                    Name of Alfred Jingle!
                    Twenty six and single—
                    More than willing to mingle.

                    All the ladies love him—
                    And strictly entre nous—
                    The ladies all admit
                    That's he's a Romeo of expert ease.

Tupman   He's a bit of a devil!

Jingle   I'm a hell of a devil!

Winkle   On any level!

Jingle   On every level!

Snodgrass   A hell of a devil

All Pickwickians On every level!

Jingle   And a bit of a character, too!

All   *Olé!*

Snodgrass Will you allow us to offer a slight mark of our esteem by begging
    the favour of your company at dinner?
Jingle Capital notion—don't presume to dictate, but broiled fowl and
    mushrooms—very good here—what time?
Snodgrass (*looking at his watch*) Let me see, it is now nearly three. Shall we
    say five?
Jingle Suit me excellently, five precisely—till then—care of yourselves.

Jingle departs, leaving the group profoundly impressed

Winkle Evidently a traveller in many countries, and a close observer of men and things.

Tupman I should like to see those girls.

Snodgrass I should like to see his poem.

Winkle I should like to have seen that dog.

Snodgrass, Winkle and Pickwick exit

Three Waiters, Sam Weller and Jingle enter

Jingle What's going forward, my man?

Sam Ball in the aid of charity, sir. Just suit you sir, by the look of your boots.

Tupman As a matter of fact, it's this very evening.

Sam Tickets at the bar, sir, half-a-guinea each, sir.

Jingle Can almost hear the company now—fiddles tuning—now the harp—there they go.

Tupman Would you like to go?

Jingle Should indeed, should indeed, but nothing to go in—odd, ain't it? Brown paper parcel here, that's all—other luggage gone by water—packing-cases, nailed up big as houses—heavy, heavy, damned heavy.

Tupman I should be very happy to lend you a change of apparell for the Ball, but you are rather slim, and I—

Jingle Rather fat—very.

Tupman (*rather annoyed*) I was about to observe, sir, that though my apparell would be too large, a jacket of my friend Mr Winkle might perhaps fit you better.

Jingle Just the thing.

Tupman Winkle won't go to the Ball—late nights are not good for his training routine, he says, but I know he has a club jacket in a carpet bag, and supposing you wore it to the Ball, and took it off when we returned, I could replace it without troubling him at all about the matter.

Jingle Capital notion—damned odd situation though, isn't it eh!—fourteen coats in the packing-cases, and obliged to wear another man's—just the thing.

Tupman (*taking out his money*) We must purchase our tickets.

Jingle Not worth splitting a guinea, toss who shall pay for both—I call, you spin.

Tupman, rather unwillingly, spins the coin. Before he can look at it, Jingle takes it

First time—heads—heads—bewitching heads.

The music for the ballroom scene begins. The set moves to ballroom position. The dancers walk on to their dancing places talking as they come. When they are all in position they start to dance. The set should be changed by this time. It is done by the men dressed as footmen. This dance is a comedy routine for Pickwick who is definitely a non-dancer!

SCENE 4   **music**

The Ballroom Of The George And Vulture

Pickwick and the Pickwickians with Wardle, Dr Slammer and Dodson and Fogg are dancing the Quadrille with Isabella, Rachel and Emily and some other ladies

Music 6. The Quadrille

During the dance the man at the door makes the following calls as appropriate to the music—the Quadrille being left flexible

Man at Door   Grand Chain Crossing
Promenade your partners
Chassé
Promenade your partners
Lady's Grand Chain Crossing
Everybody gallop
And repeat.
Grand Chain Crossing
Leading couples advance and retire
Advance to garland
And chassé
Promenade your partners
Gallop
Grand Chain Crossing
Honour your partners.

The dancers break up and promenade the room talking, and some go out on to the terrace. A flying piece comes in downstage—a series of arches right across the stage—which separates the exterior terrace from the ballroom proper and allows the dialogue to progress with a minimum of background action. All dialogue is played on this terrace

Tupman Not at all bad. You *do* look like Winkle in that jacket—that's the first to be made with our club button.
Jingle Really? (*Looking at the button.*) P.C. and the old fellow's likeness—what does P.C. stand for?—peculiar coat, eh?
Man at Door Sir Thomas and Lady Clubber and Miss Caroline Clubber.

Tupman and Jingle observe Miss Caroline Clubber

Tupman (*very taken with her*) My word, how's that for a fine young filly!
Jingle (*airily*) Caroline Clubber—the Cumberland Clubbers. Father vast
fortune from betting, beef and breweries. Easy money for him—easy
virtue for her. Popular saying—"Join the Clubbers". Be careful—very.
Tupman (*nodding knowingly*) She sounds a little risque to me. I'm the more
ardent type. Devoted. Loyal.
Jingle Sounds like a cocker spaniel.
Tupman Love, thy name is Rachel!

Tupman goes to find Rachel

Jingle lingers below stairs to listen to Wardle and Pickwick

Pickwick Drink your punch, Wardle. You're very edgy tonight.
Wardle It's my sister Rachel, you know—for ever telling all and sundry
how much she's worth. The first bright prospector who comes along will
relieve her of the lot. (*To the Fat Boy.*) Joe, keep an eye on Miss Rachel—
now stay awake, damn you, and keep an eye on her.

The Fat Boy goes to sleep against one of the arches

    Jingle leaves

Pickwick It's all right for you, Wardle, I've got three of them to keep an
eye on.
Wardle Sisters?
Pickwick Club members, sir. They're very fresh tonight—it's the mating
season, you know.
Wardle Damn it, Pickwick, they're only boys.
Pickwick Damn it, sir, that's not the point, you know what boys are!
Wardle Well, I know what *girls* are! . . .
Pickwick Well, put them together and what do you get?

Pickwick and Wardle leave

Snodgrass and Emily come through the arches on to the terrace

Emily I think your verse charming, Mr Snodgrass—
Snodgrass Thank you.
Emily —but do you write nothing of a more . . . *exciting* nature?
Snodgrass For you, Miss Emily, I would essay any excitement—just name
it, sweet lady.
Emily Blood sports!
Snodgrass (*rather put off*) Oh, yes, the poetry of nature.
Emily I simply love cub-hunting.
Snodgrass Oh, yes, indeed! Adorable little creatures—so fluffy and full of
fun.

Emily The cry of the hounds, Mr Snodgrass, sets my skin a-tingle.
Snodgrass Indeed, Miss Emily, I know exactly what you mean.
Emily It's so frightfully exciting to course a hare.
Snodgrass Absolutely thrilling, Miss Emily.

Pickwick and Wardle appear through the arches

Pickwick What! What! What!
Emily Ah! Mr Snodgrass was just telling me about his poems, Papa.
Wardle Good, good—nothing like poetry to take your mind off other things!
Pickwick And you, sir.
Snodgrass Miss Emily was extolling the glories of the hunt, sir.
Pickwick Very good! Nothing like violent exercise for the young and frisky, eh! What! What! Nothing like punch for the more mature.

Pickwick and Wardle make to go off

Snodgrass and Emily go back into the ballroom

Rachel and Tupman come onto the terrace

Tupman (*to Rachel*) Will you permit me—
Pickwick (*turning back*) What! What! What!
Tupman —er, to explain the lofty principles of our divine club!
Pickwick Oh, yes, very good, carry on. I'm watching you, watching!

Pickwick and Wardle go off through the arches

Jingle comes back to eavesdrop

Tupman Your digits are irresistible—will you permit me? (*He takes Rachel's hand*)
Rachel Oh, Mr Tupman, do you not think that my dear nieces are far prettier?
Tupman I should if their aunt were not here, and I dazzled by her brilliance.
Rachel Oh! You naughty, naughty man.
Tupman Naughty is as naughty does.
Rachel If only their complexions were a little better.
Tupman I am hypnotized by the pure white alabaster of their impregnable aunt.
Rachel Oh! You quiz—but I know what you were going to say.
Tupman You do? Well, whisper those sweet surrendering words into my eager ears.
Rachel You were going to say that you don't think that Isabella's stooping is as bad as Emily's boldness.
Tupman Miss Wardle, Miss Wardle, compared to them you are an angel with wings of crimson flame. I am tinder to your fire—burn me, madam!

Rachel Men are such deceivers.

The Fat Boy wakes up and sees Rachel and Tupman kissing and jumps up

Fat Boy Cor, blimey!
Rachel Mr Tupman, we're observed, we're discovered!

Rachel rushes off through the arches and joins Dr Slammer. Tupman goes to follow but Jingle stops him

Jingle Fat boy will tell brother—pursuit not advisable.
Tupman What am I to do?
Jingle Avert suspicion—pay attention to niece Isabella—I'll pretend to pursue Rachel—put everybody on the wrong scent.
Tupman Who's she talking to now?
Jingle Pompous doctor—after money. Don't worry, I'll get rid of him—now pursue Isabella.
Tupman My dear fellow, what a wonderful idea! How can I ever repay you?
Jingle Lend me five pounds.
Tupman (*looking in his wallet*) I only have ten!
Jingle (*taking it*) That will do beautifully—Isabella!

Tupman goes through the arches and goes to talk to Isabella. Jingle walks into the ballroom towards Dr Slammer and Rachel, pushes the doctor's hat down over his eyes and grabs Rachel by the arm, pulling her on to the terrace

Rachel Oh, Doctor—Doctor Slammer—you are a quiz! Oh! Oh!
Jingle Miss Wardle, must tell you—
Dr Slammer (*coming on to the terrace*) Sir, sir, my name is Slammer—Dr Slammer, ninety-seventh Regiment Chatham Barracks—my card, sir—my card.
Jingle Ah! Slammer—much obliged—polite attention—not ill now, Slammer—when I am, knock you up.
Slammer Sir, you're a shuffler, a poltroon, a coward and a liar!
Jingle Yes.
Slammer Will nothing induce you to give me your card?
Jingle Ah! I see, drink too strong—lemonade much better—suffer for it in the morning.
Slammer Sir, you're intoxicated now, sir. You're stopping in this house, sir, but you shall hear from me in the morning, I shall find you out, sir. I shall find you out.
Jingle Rather you found me out than found me in.
Slammer Insufferable young puppy!

Dr Slammer goes off in a rage through the arches

Jingle Miss Wardle, forgive intrusion—short acquaintance—no time for ceremony—must tell you—bad news—Tupman only wants you for your money.

Rachel He wants *me*!

Jingle No, no, your money!

Rachel The wretch! ,

Jingle More than that—loves another!

Rachel Another—who?

Jingle Short girl—blonde hair—Isabella.

Rachel It can't be. I won't believe it.

Jingle You watch him.

Rachel I will.

Despite herself Rachel looks at Tupman who does indeed seem to be making up to Isabella

Jingle Watch his looks.

Rachel I will.

Jingle His whispers.

Rachel I will.

Jingle He'll stand next to her.

Rachel Let him.

Jingle He'll flatter her.

Rachel Let him.

Jingle He'll pay her every possible attention.

Rachel Let him!

Jingle turns Rachel from the distressing sight of Tupman and Isabella

Jingle And he'll cut *you*!

Rachel Cut *me*! *Will* he!

Jingle Miss Wardle, don't you realise you need someone who loves you for yourself?

Rachel Yes.

Jingle Your character.

Rachel Yes.

Jingle Your beauty.

Rachel Yes.

Jingle Your *money*—would mean nothing to somebody who really loved you.

Rachel Yes, but *who* for instance?

Jingle Me!

Rachel (*melting*) Oh, Mr Jingle, sir.

music   **Music 7. Song: There's Something About You**

Jingle sings to Rachel, Snodgrass to Emily and Tupman to Isabella

Jingle   There's something about you.
                          What can it be?—
                          To cause that pounding sound I hear
                          Whenever you're near to me.

Tupman   Is it the rich, cool colour of your eyes,
                          Or the bewitching way
                          In which they hypnotise me?

Snodgrass   There's something about you—
                          This much I know.
                          Money could never buy
                          That kind of glow.

Jingle ⎫   Whatever your magic may be,
Tupman ⎬   I can never be without you—
Snodgrass ⎭   For there's something about you
                          For me.

Jingle   There's something about you—
Rachel   What can it be?
Jingle   To cause this pounding sound I hear
                          Whenever you're near to me.

                          Is it the rich, cool colour of your eyes?
                          Or the bewitching way
                          In which they hypnotise me?

Jingle   There's something about you—
Rachel   This much I know!
Jingle   Money! . . . could never buy
                          That kind of glow.
                          Whatever your magic may be,
                          I can never be without you—
                          For there's something about you
                          For me.

*Jingle starts systematically to remove Rachel's jewellery during the second
part of this number. He takes her necklace and earrings, examines each with
a jeweller's glass before pocketing it. He finishes by cutting the strings of her
purse with a pair of scissors. She is blissfully unaware that her money is all
that interests him*

Jingle   There's something about you—

Rachel	What can it be?
Jingle	I look at you and see
Rachel	A land of fable and fantasy.
Jingle	Is it the wealth . . . of wisdom in your smile?
	Or just the stealthy way
	In which your smile beguiles me?
	There's something about you—
Rachel	This I can see!
Jingle	Diamonds . . . could never have—
Rachel	—sparkle like me!
Jingle	Whatever your magic may be,
	I can never be without you!—
	For there's something about you
	For me.
All	Whatever your magic may be,
	I can never be without you,
	For there's something about you
	Some special something about you,
	For me.

There's something about you
What can it be?
I look at you and see a land
Of fable and fantasy.
Is it the wealth of wisdom
In your smile.

Or just the stealthy way
In which your smile beguiles me.

As the chorus sing, the dancers dance and the scenery changes to Pickwick's bedroom. The number ends as the change is completed and the lights come up on the new scene

There's something about you,
This much I know
Money could never buy
That kind of glow
Whatever your magic may be
I can never be without you
For there's something about you
Yes, there is something about you
Some special something about you
For me.

SCENE 5

Pickwick's Chambers

There is a bed LC and a harmonium UL

Mary is tidying up. Sam comes in and whistles at her

Mary Did you say something, or is the wind blowing a Christmas carol on that great big fat lickorish nose of yours?

Sam That face! That apparitious vision! Them eyes—them limpid orbs of currulium blue. That form divine! That lissom step, light-footed like a fairy in a cabbage patch. You're the new chamber-maid, ain't you, girl?

Mary Cor!

Sam Cor! Oh, you eloquacious fowl! Don't I just know what I would like to give *you* for Christmas! Where's Mr Pickwick?

Mary Is he the one who's in here—oh—he didn't come in last night. He's still upstairs drinking in Mr Wardle's room.

Sam What's your name, girl?

Mary Mary.

Sam No, it can't be. Samivel Veller, you're doomed yet again. I hope.

Mary How's that, then

Sam Better not speak. Better just bear it. Better suffer in silence what no human female can alleviate.

Mary All right then, don't tell me.

Sam All right then, I will. That name has caused a small flame of trust to leap up in my wounded breast.

Mary What, Mary?

Sam Marys have, since boyhood, been flame to my flax.

Mary You can't half talk, mate.

Sam I can, girl.

Mrs Bardell (*off*) Sam!

Mary Talk on, then, mate. Talk never popped no 'taters in the oven.

Sam No, but it helps to blow up a good hot fire to roast them by.

Mrs Bardell enters

Mrs Bardell Sam, you lazy, idle, *lecherous* lump! Why don't you answer when I call?

Sam Wouldn't be genteel to answer till you done talking.

Mrs Bardell Number twenty-two wants his boots.

Sam Will he have 'em now or wait till he gets 'em?

Mrs Bardell (*to Mary*) And you, you get on about your business and don't dilly dally with 'im or it won't just be your boots that'll get polished.

Mrs Bardell bustles out

Sam Scurvy old crow! Who's number twenty-two to put all the others out?
I'm getting out of this, I am.

Mary You'll not be leaving the old *George and Vulture* so soon after we've
been introduced, I hope.

Sam Don't you worry, girl, you'll be attended to. I'm seeing after a job
with these 'ere Pickwickians.

Mary You don't want to 'ave nothing to do with strolling players, mate.

Sam The Pickwick Club, girl! Them happy band of bachelor brothers up
there in Mr Wardle's room, swilling of their old port and making of their
fine mendacious speeches. Gentlemen, the lot of them, you can tell by the
way they 'old their drink.

Mary I bet you could teach them a thing or two when it comes to that.

Sam I bet I could teach *you* a thing or two when it comes to that. (*He slips
his arm around her*). Experience, my girl is what counts, experience!

Mary insincerely makes to get away

Music 8. Song: Learn A Little Something   music

When I was only four years old,
Me pore ole father
Upped and told me
"Sammy" he said
Wiv a claht rahnd the 'ead,
He said, "Ere you are
Laying about,
When you should be out there
Earning a living
Giving instead er taking the bread
From the pore old marth er yer
Dear old muvver 'n me."
So, seein' as 'ow
Me dear ole father
Was indisputably right,
The wery next night
I puts on me boots
And off I scoots
From our 'umble 'ovel
Ter grovel 'n' cheat
'N' steal in the street
In degradation 'n' squalor.
That's Chapter One
Of the funny story
Of 'ow I become a scholar!

And though I don't profess ter be
A professor nor a preacher,

There is one thing I 'ave learned in life—
Experience is a bloody fine teacher!

	Every day we learn a little sumfin'—
Mary	Learn a little sumfin' new.
Sam	One day it may be the A.B.C.
Mary	Next day that one and one make two—
	And not three!
Sam	Every day we learn another lesson.
Mary	Learn another lesson now.
Sam }	However clever you may be—
Mary	Be your knowledge great or small—
Sam	The best in school—
Mary	Or just a fool—
Both	No one knows it all!
Sam	Cos every day the world's a little diff'rent.
Mary	Things are changing every way.
Sam }	And there's no one yet
Mary	Been born, I'll bet,
	Who'll deny it's true to say
	We learn a little sumfin' every day.

Every day we learn a little sumfin'—
Learn a little sumfin' more,
One day it may be some fancy tricks—
Next day that two and two make four—
And not six!

Every day we grow a little wiser—
Wiser than the day before.
For every hour our minds expand
And improve in every way.
So twenty-four means plenty more
Wisdom every day.

Sam	Every day we gain a grain of knowledge—
Mary	College days are here to stay.
Sam }	And there's no one yet
Mary	Been born, I'll bet
	Who'll deny it's true to say,
	We learn a little sumfin' every day.

Dance

You and me,
Brainy though we may be,
We learn a little sumfin' every day.

Pickwick enters

Sam sees Pickwick and hustles Mary off

Pickwick (*singing*) There's something about you?
Sam The werry top of the morning to you, sir.
Pickwick And the top of the stairs to you, sir; who are you?
Sam Sam Veller, sir. Remember me, sir?
Pickwick How's the candle business?
Sam Werry waxy, sir, I'm the fellow—
Pickwick I remember you, how you've changed. When I think what a fine tall fellow you used to be.
Sam I was standing on a ladder at the time, sir.
Pickwick So you were. Fixing the window. How much do I owe you?
Sam Not a ha'penny, unless you hire me, sir.
Pickwick But I don't need a cab just now.
Sam Just as well, sir. I don't have one.
Pickwick Your nose is familiar, sir. You're Jackson Scurvey's brother, by Jove!
Sam I'm Tony Veller's son by someone.
Pickwick Veller?
Sam Werry. And how are you in yourself, sir?
Pickwick As "weller" as can be expected. I've been drinking with old Wardle. I could do with a servant, though.
Sam I think I know someone, sir. (*He takes off Pickwick's gaiters*)
Pickwick How's your present situation?
Sam Not so good as your'n, sir. What's the wages?
Pickwick Twelve pounds a year.
Sam Clothes?
Pickwick Two suits.
Sam Work?
Pickwick To attend upon myself and other honourable members of the Pickwick Club.
Sam I'm let. And the terms is agreed upon.
Pickwick You accept the situation?
Sam Of course.
Pickwick You can get a character?
Sam Of course, sir, I *am* a character! Ask the landlady of the *White Hart* about that, sir. And if she lies, ask the landlady of the *Belle Savage*, and if she's dumb, ask the landlady of the *King's Arms*, the *Queen's Head*, the *Leg O'Mutton*, the *Seven Stars*, the *Three Bottles*, the *Two Partridges*. There's only one Sam Veller, sir.

Music 9. Song: You've Never Met A Feller Like Me   music

Sam
I'll bet you've never met a feller like me, sir.
Clever as a monkey up a banyan tree, sir.
Any problem—you name it—
Just aim it at little old me.

Never in all your born days—
Never in all your vie—
Have you ever met a feller
Like young Sam Weller—
No, you never met a feller like me!

I can tell you stories that'll make you smile;
I know bags of barmaids that are well worth while.
Down the Strand, there's a tavern called *The Pretty
Pickle*
Play your cards right, barmaid likes a bit of slap and
tickle.
I know every barmaid out to Notting Hill—
Lots of barmaids won't—but a lot more will!
Oh, the thrill of being well-informed—well, you can
plainly see
It pays to know an influential feller like me.

I'll bet you never met a feller like me, sir.
Clever and as nippy as a circus flea, sir.
Any trouble—you name it—
Just blame it on little ole me.

Quick as a flash I'll fix it—
Quick as the eye can see.
'Cos you never met a feller
Like young Sam Weller—
No, you never met a feller like me!

Pickwick Just a minute, Sam—there's something *you* ought to know!
I'll bet you never met a feller like me, Sam,
Clever sort of feller with the brains of three, Sam.
Brain as big as my belly;
Intelligent to a degree!

People who hardly know me
Readily all agree,
That they never met a feller
Like me, Sam Weller;
No! they never met a feller like me!

I have secrets men would not impart;
Sam (*speaking*) Go on, Sir—tell us!
Pickwick   London's horse bus routes—I know 'em all by heart!
Sam (*speaking*) You wicked old devil, Sir!
Pickwick   People say "It's amazing!" Can't think what all the fuss
is!
I just have this talent for remembering the buses!

	I know every bus stop out of Kentish Town; People ask me, "How ?" Well! I wrote them down! Oh! the crown of wisdom fits me well; How fine it is to be a worthwhile Thinking educated fellow like me!
Sam	I'll bet you never met a feller like me, Sir, I can bend me 'ead until I touch my knee, Sir.
Pickwick	So can I, Sam!
Sam	Let's see yer! (*Business*)
Sam ⎤ Pickwick ⎦	Never in living memory,—never in history———! (Sam Weller—) Have they met a feller like me, (Sir,———) No! they never met a feller like me———!
Sam	I know how to dance the latest dance! (*He does so!*)
Pickwick	I can name the Minister of War for France———! I can recall who was present at the Coronation!
Sam	Strikes me, Sir! you're quite a mine of useless information! I can turn a cartwheel! (*He does so!*)
Pickwick	Oh! Well! so can I———!
Sam	Can you, Sir?
Pickwick	Of course!
Sam	Then, let's see you try!

Music stops as Pickwick removes his jacket and turns a cartwheel!

Sam ⎤ Pickwick ⎦	Oh! the sky's the limit And the net result is genius plus! For two fantastic fellers like us!
Pickwick	It's true you never met a feller like me, Sam. Clever as a feller with a Ph.D., Sam!

Music stops

Sam (*speaking*) What's that, Sir?
Pickwick (*speaking*) Ph.D.?—It stands for Pickwickian Horticultural Diploma!
Sam (*speaking*) Oh!

Pickwick	Intellectual—discerning— And burning with learning,—that's me! Why don't I just admit it? Modest though I be; That you never met a feller like me, Sam Weller, No! you never, ever, met a clever feller like me———! Me———!
Sam	Me———! (*a higher note*)
Pickwick	Me———! (*higher*)
Sam	Me———! (*higher*)
Pickwick	Me———! (*top note*)

Sam gives up. They shake hands!

Pickwick Sam Weller. I knew you all the time. You're hired.
Sam At last I am a gentleman's gentleman.
Pickwick I shall make suitable arrangements for you immediately. Mind
you, Mrs Bardell is a little short of staff—do you think that Mrs Bardell
is likely to let you leave your present situation? I shall have to handle this
very diplomatically, Sam. (*He starts making preparations for bed—cleaning
teeth, gargling, etc. He has unbuttoned his trousers*)
Sam Yes, she's a real stickler, sir, but no one can manage her better nor
you, can they, sir?
Pickwick (*wheezing*) Went down the wrong way. How will I go about asking
Mrs Bardell? I mean she might not want to let you go. I've got it, I've
got it. Mrs Bardell.
Sam Yes, sir.
Pickwick Your little boy is a very long time gone.
Sam Well, it's a good long way to the Market, sir.
Pickwick Has her little boy gone to the Market?
Sam I dare say so, sir.
Pickwick Mrs Bardell, about your man, Weller.
Sam Sir! A werry pertinacious and altogether charming fellow.
Pickwick Very good! Mrs Bardell, don't you think that I might find it a
greater expense to keep two people than to keep one?
Sam No, sir.
Pickwick In that case, Mrs Bardell—

Mrs Bardell enters carrying a breakfast tray

Mrs Bardell Yes, sir.
Pickwick Mrs Bardell!
Mrs Bardell Breakfast, sir.

Sam slips out before Mrs Bardell sees him

Pickwick (*doing up his trousers in a great hurry*) What! What! What!
Mrs Bardell The chops and tomato sauce, sir.
Pickwick (*feeling ill*) Oh, no.
Mrs Bardell Yes, sir. Just as you ordered, sir. As ever, sir, always at your
service, yours sincerely, Mrs Bardell. I've done a little reply to your note
of last night, sir. It's under the cover, sir, done up like a frill round the
base of the biggest chop, sir.
Pickwick Won't the tomato sauce stain it?
Mrs Bardell I don't care, sir, it was worth it.
Pickwick Mrs Bardell.
Mrs Bardell Yes, sir.
Pickwick Your little boy is a very long time gone.
Mrs Bardell Gone, sir?
Pickwick He has gone to the Market, hasn't he?

Mrs Bardell No, sir, he's playing in the yard, sir.

Pickwick Playing in the yard. Start again! Mrs Bardell, don't you think that I might find it a greater expense to keep two people than to keep one?

Mrs Bardell *(coyly)* La, Mr Pickwick, what a question!

Pickwick What's your feeling, madam?

Mrs Bardell Very tender, Mr Pickwick.

Pickwick What about expense, though?

Mrs Bardell That depends, if it's a saving and careful person, sir.

Pickwick True, true. The person I have in my eyes I think possesses these qualities.

Mrs Bardell How kind of you, sir.

Pickwick Such a person, Mrs Bardell, could be of material use to me.

Mrs Bardell La, Mr Pickwick.

Pickwick To tell you the truth—Mrs Bardell, I have made up my mind.

Mrs Bardell Oh, sir!

Pickwick No doubt you think it strange now that I haven't mentioned this matter to you before.

Mrs Bardell Bachelor gentlemen 'as their little ways, sir.

Pickwick *(a little out of his depth)* Quite. And what is your conclusion, madam?

Mrs Bardell Oh, Mr Pickwick, you're very kind, sir.

Pickwick It'll cause you a good deal of trouble, won't it?

Mrs Bardell Oh, I've never thought anything of the trouble, sir, and of course I shall take more trouble than ever to please you then, sir.

Pickwick How considerate you are, Mrs Bardell!

Mrs Bardell How considerate *you* are, Mr Pickwick, sir!

Pickwick And as for your little boy—

Mrs Bardell Bless him.

Pickwick He'll have a companion, too—

Mrs Bardell Bless you.

Pickwick A lively one, I guarantee.

Mrs Bardell I am sure you'll teach us a trick or two, Mr Pickwick.

Pickwick It's agreed between us then, madam.

Mrs Bardell Oh, yes, sir, it is, sir.

Pickwick I'm much relieved, madam and deeply grateful.

Mrs Bardell Oh, no, sir, it's *me* that 'as to be relieved and grateful, sir!

Music 10. Song Option

Directors may choose which of the following two numbers they include in their production, either Look Into Your Heart *(used in the original production) or* I'll Never Be Lonely Again *(written for a revival)*

Option 1

Pickwick I appreciate deeply your understanding that a man cannot live alone for ever, doing for himself.

Mrs Bardell I'll do for you, sir. It'll be one long duet, sir, just like our musical evenings together. And so much more time to practise. (*She goes to the harmonium*)
Pickwick Mrs Bardell, this is hardly the time.
Mrs Bardell Oh, come on, sir. Just one quick chorus together, sir. (*She sits at the harmonium, and plays the introduction*)
Pickwick All right—four bars in—Look Into Your Heart.

music   **Music 10: Look Into Your Heart**

     (*Singing*)   Look into your heart
                          And what you see
                          You must believe.

                          Know what's in your heart
                          Don't wear your heart
                          Upon your sleeve.

                          Life is a game
                          Seldom the same
                          Who knows what's in store?
                          We don't keep the score.

                          Search into your heart
                          For in your heart
                          You'll find the truth.

                          Truth as rare as fame
                          As bright as flame
                          As sweet as youth.

                          Yours to use
                          Or refuse
                          Only you can choose—
                          Just look into your heart.

Bardell	**Pickwick**
Look into your heart	Look into your heart
And what you see	Look into your heart
You must believe	And when you do you must believe
	What you see there.
Know what's in your heart	Know your heart
Don't wear your heart	Every part

Upon your sleeve   Know it well for there's a lot to
                                          see there

                                          Life is a game
                                          Seldom the same.

Both   Who knows what's in store?
                  We don't keep the score.

Pickwick   **Bardell**
Search into your heart   Search into your heart
For in your heart   Search into your heart
You'll find the truth   Somewhere in your heart
                                          That is where the truth is.

Bardell   **Pickwick**
Truth as rare as fame   Rare as fame
As bright as flame   Bright as flame
As sweet as youth   For the truth is
                                          Quite as sweet as youth is.

Pickwick   **Bardell**
Yours to use   Yours. Yours
Or refuse   Yours. Yours
Only you can choose   Just take a little look into your
Just look into your heart   heart.

*Mrs Bardell flings her arms about Pickwick's neck, overcome with joyful
tears*

Option 2

Pickwick I appreciate deeply your understanding that a man cannot live
   alone for ever, doing for himself.
Mrs Bardell Don't worry, sir—I'll do for you.

Music 10: I'll Never Be Lonely Again   music

(*In which Pickwick sings of Sam Weller, and Mrs Bardell of Pickwick*)

Pickwick   I'll have someone to love and care for me—
                      Someone with time to spare for me—

Someone who's always there for me
When
I need someone to say
That I am the nicest of men—
I'll never be lonely again.

Mrs Bardell You'll have someone to walk your way with you—
Someone to spend your day with you—
Someone who wants to stay with you
When ...
Pickwick All I wish for's
An evening spent by the fireside
And then ...
While I tune my lyre up—
And you build my fire up—
I'll never be lonely again!

Mrs Bardell (*with mounting enthusiasm*) Oh, and there's more, Mr Pickwick! So *much* more!

(*Singing*) You'll have someone to wash your hair for you—
Prepare the fairest fare for you—
Care for your underwear for you
When ...
Pickwick I need someone to prove
That I'm the most pampered of men—
Both I'll never be lonely again!
Mrs Bardell You'll have someone who'll sew and mend for you—
Someone who'll always fend for you—
Someone who'll be a friend for you
When
Pickwick When like Daniel I stand alone
With the lion in its den—
I'll never be lonely—
Mrs Bardell Life's lovely if only—
Pickwick I'll never be lonely again!

Mrs Bardell (*speaking*) Not if I 'ave anything to do with it, you won't, sir!
(*Singing*) I'll have someone to warm the hearth for me—
Someone to plan the path for me—
Pickwick Someone to run the bath for me—
Then
I shall live like the kings in Biblical days did—
Mrs Bardell Amen!
Both I'll never be lonely again!

Mrs Bardell I'll have someone who'll take control for me—
Someone who'll sell his soul for me—
Pickwick Someone who'll carry coal for me—
Then

	When it's Christmas
	And good King Wenceslas looks out again,
	At last I'll be suited—
Mrs Bardell	That's quite undisputed!—
	And I'm so excited!
Pickwick	My dear, I'm delighted!
Both	We'll never be lonely again!

*Mrs Bardell flings her arms about Pickwick's neck, overcome with joyful
tears*

Mrs Bardell My good man, sir, my lovely, dear, good, lovely man—

Pickwick collapses on to the bed, Mrs Bardell on top of him

I'll never leave you, sir, it's chops and tomato sauce for you for ever, sir,
on the house, sir. (*She kisses him heartily*)

Pickwick No, no—somebody's coming up the stairs. (*He tries to free himself
and eventually succeeds*)

*Pickwick has heard the approach of Tupman, Winkle, Snodgrass and Sam
coming upstairs. At the same time, Georgie rushes into the room, pushing
past them*

Georgie I want my mum. Where's my mum? (*Louder*) I want 'er. I don't
want you. I want my mum. (*He charges like a bullet into Pickwick, whom
he commences to butt, hit and pinch violently*) What are you doing to her?
Mrs Bardell It's all right, Georgie, Uncle Samuel is not hurting Mummy.

Sam Weller arrives

Sam holds Georgie. Mrs Bardell faints back on to the bed

Snodgrass Well!
Winkle Yes.
Tupman Quite.

Georgie frees himself from Sam and runs down the stairs, yelling

Georgie (*as he goes*) He's done her in! He's knocked her off! 'E's pulverised
her! He's murdered me mum!
Sam That's torn it.
Pickwickians (*pointing to Pickwick's trouser flap*) Mr Pickwick, sir Mr
Pickwick, etc.
Sam I take it, sir, that Madam was overwhelmed with the effort of carrying

that heavy tray up all of them stairs. Why she will do it I do not know. 'Ow very kind of you, sir, to convey her to your couch and administer Sal Wolatile, artificial desperation and other revivalist methods. But do not fret yourself further. We'll all help you to—

music	**Music 10A. Song: Talk (reprise)**
(Singing)	Talk your way out of it

Talk your way out of it
Talk your way out of it
Talk around about a bit.
But talk.

You're in a tight old corner.

Talk your way out of it
Talk your way out of it
Talk around about a bit
But talk.

Or she'll be Mrs Pickwick.

Talk your way out of it
Talk your way out of it
Talk around about a bit.
But talk.

After the reprise they all exit, Tupman and Sam carrying the unconscious Mrs Bardell

Mr Winkle and Mr Snodgrass are detained by two officers in dress uniform who appear at the doorway

Officer Mr Winkle, I presume?
Winkle Why yes, sir. My name is Winkle.
Officer You will not be surprised, sir, when I inform you that I have called here this morning on behalf of my friend, Dr Slammer of the Ninety-seventh.
Winkle Dr Slammer!
Officer Dr Slammer. He begged me to express his opinion that your conduct of last evening was of a description which no gentleman could endure, and in consequence of your firm refusal to give your card to Dr Slammer, I was desired by that gentleman to identify the wearer of a very uncommon coat—a bright blue dress coat with silver buttons displaying a bust and the letters "P.C."

Winkle looks at his coat in astonishment. The officer slaps his face with a glove

(*In careless tone*) Shall we say—sunset this evening? You know Fort Pitt? If you will take the trouble to turn into the field which borders on to the river, take the footpath to the left and keep straight on till you see me, I will precede you to a secluded place, where the affair can be conducted without fear of interruption. Nothing more to arrange, I think. Good morning. Good morning.

The Officers leave

Winkle is devastated

Winkle Good morning. It *must* be me, Snodgrass. I took too much wine for dinner. The fact is, I was very drunk, and this message is the terrible result.
Snodgrass I will attend you.
Winkle The consequences may be dreadful.
Snodgrass I hope not.
Winkle Dr Slammer of the Ninety-seventh. He must be a very good shot.
Snodgrass Well, so are you, ain't you?
Winkle Yes. Snodgrass, do not let me be baulked in this matter—do not give information to the local authorities—do not obtain the assistance of several peace officers, to take either me or Dr Slammer of the Ninety-seventh Regiment at present quartered in Chatham Barracks, into custody, and thus prevent this duel—I say, do *not*!
Snodgrass (*seizing Winkle's hand warmly; enthusiastically*) *Not* for worlds!

Winkle looks tragic

SCENE 6

Music 10B. The Duel   music

A comical dirge-like march begins as Snodgrass and Winkle walk slowly towards the duelling ground. The setting changes as they walk to a field by a frozen river. Winkle takes a swig of brandy

Dr Slammer, a Surgeon and the Officers, as Seconds, are there

One of the Officers approaches in the same formal manner as before. He opens a pistol case and offers it to Winkle for him to make his choice

Sinister music plays quietly under

Officer (*approaching Snodgrass*) Excuse me, sir, but do you persist in allowing your puny little friend to commit suicide?

Snodgrass (*horrified*) S-s-s-suicide? I-I—
Officer You are aware, I have no doubt, of Dr Slammer's fearsome repu-
tation upon the field of death?
Winkle (*overhearing*) F-f-f-f-field of d-death?

*Snodgrass and Winkle listen in mounting horror as the Officer describes
Slammer in a voice filled with basso-profundo menace*

The Pickwickians (*reprise*) and Talk (*reprise*)

Officer   Picture if you can
                       This indestructible man—
                       Understatement will tell you
                       He's sadistic and cruel—
                       And I don't like to tell you
                       What he's like in a duel!

                       Nonpareil to say the least—
                       All his friends call him "The Beast"!
                       He will blow a man to pieces
                       With a cheerful smile—
                       He thinks of killing as a feast!

Winkle
Snodgrass } (*together gulping*) A *feast*?!
Officer   (*nodding*) That's Slammer! That's Slammer!
                       Beyond a disembowelling doubt, that's Slammer!!
                       A man who loves to tear opponents limb from limb—
                       Dr "Deathhead" Slammer—
                       That's him!

                       Murderous and merciless—
                       Callous and cruel—
                       The quickest way to Hell's
                       To face him in a duel!
                       (*Looking at Winkle*) You poor, dead fool!

Winkle (*in a small voice, to Snodgrass*) Snodgrass, I have a sudden, very
sensible idea!
Snodgrass (*beside himself*) What, what, what?
Winkle   I ought to
                       Talk my way out of it!
                       Talk my way out of it—
                       Talk around about a bit—
                       But talk!
Officer   (*smiling*) Or you'll be rotting corpses!
Snodgrass   (*screaming*) Talk your way out of it!
Both   Talk our way out of it!
                       Talk around about a bit—
                       But talk!

Snodgrass   (*wailing*) But how!
Officer   It's too late! Slammer is furious at the delay!
                     He wants blood!
Winkle   (*shaking*) B-b-blood? Oh, dear God!

*Winkle takes a pistol out of the box, passes it to Snodgrass who passes it back.
Winkle puts the pistol back in the box. The Officer hands Winkle a pistol
firmly. Winkle points the pistol straight at Snodgrass who pushes the barrel
away from himself. The Officer crosses to Dr Slammer and hands him a pistol.
The two contestants take off their cloaks. At a signal from the Seconds, they
begin to walk towards each other. They reach each other, turn about and wait.
The Second gives a signal and they laboriously pace six paces away from each
other and take aim. Winkle's pistol shakes violently. It goes off accidentally
and frightens him so much he falls to the ground*

A pheasant falls from the flies

Snodgrass (*confused*) G-g-good shot!

*Snodgrass and the Surgeon rush to Winkle's aid. Dr Slammer walks over to
inspect the damage*

Slammer That's not the man!
Second Not the man?
Snodgrass Not the man?
Slammer Certainly not! That's not the person who insulted me last night!
Officer Most extraordinary!
Winkle I am not the person. I know it.
Slammer Why did you not communicate this fact to me, sir?
Winkle Because, sir, I have the honour, not only to wear, but to have
created the uniform, sir, of the Pickwick Club. The honour of that uniform
I felt bound to maintain, and I therefore, without inquiry, accepted the
challenge which you offered me.
Slammer (*good-humouredly advancing with extended hand*) My dear sir, I
honour your gallantry.
Winkle Thank you, sir, thank you.

Suddenly the whole party arrives to skate on the frozen river

Isabella spots Winkle on the ground

Isabella Why, what is the matter with Mr Winkle?
Wardle Don't be frightened.
Isabella (*screaming*) What's the matter?
Snodgrass Mr Winkle has met with an accident, that's all.

*Isabella utters piercing screams and drops her skates. She kneels down by
Winkle*

Wardle Throw some cold water over her.
Isabella (*recovering immediately*) No, no, I am better now. Father—Emily—
a surgeon! Is he wounded? Is he dead? Is he—ha, ha, ha! (*She becomes
hysterical*)
Winkle Calm yourself, dear; dear, calm yourself.
Isabella Then you are not dead! Oh, say you are not dead!
Wardle Don't be a fool, Isabella. What the devil's the use of saying he isn't
dead!
Winkle No, no, I am not. I require no assistance but yours. (*Whispering*)
May I put my arm around your shoulder? Oh, Miss Isabella!
Isabella Oh! Dear—dear—Mr Winkle.
Winkle (*jumping up*) Oh, say those words again! Repeat them if you would
have me recover, repeat them!
Wardle We've come down here to skate. Let's get on with it. You skate, of
course, Pickwick?
Pickwick Oh yes, I—I—am rather out of practice.
Emily Oh, do skate, Mr Pickwick, I'd like to see it so much.
Pickwick So would I—but I haven't brought my skates with me.
Tupman Well, I have two pairs. Here you are, Pickwick.

music   **Music 11. The Winter Waltz**

*Music 11 is played under the libretto, with optional background chorus (words
in Vocal Score)*

Pickwick and Co. put on skates

Winkle Well, I suppose we must take the ladies round for a turn or two.
Tupman Yes, indeed; we must hold them very tight.
Snodgrass But supposing we start to fall?
Tupman We shall simply have to hold on tighter.
Winkle But supposing *they* start to fall?
Tupman Damn it, gentlemen, can't three gentlemen and three ladies contrive
to fall together in a somewhat pleasurable manner? (*He laughs*)
Emily Where's Aunt Rachel?
Isabella She said she would come down later.
Winkle Hard luck, Tuppy.
Snodgrass Never mind, Tuppy.

Winkle and Snodgrass exit with Emily and Isabella to skate

Pickwick Severe weather, Sam.
Sam Fine time for them as is well wrapped up, as the polar bear said ven
he was practising his skating.
Pickwick (*trembling*) This ice is damn slippery.
Sam That's not uncommon.

Pickwick (*staggering*) These skates are blasted awkward.

Sam I'm afeerd there's a orkard gen'l'man in 'em.

Wardle Come now, Pickwick, the ladies are all anxiety.

Pickwick (*with a ghastly smile*) Just doing some figure skating, Wardle—look—eleven! (*Clinging round Sam's neck*) I've got two old coats at home, Sam—you may have them both.

Sam Thank 'ee, sir.

Pickwick Now we're getting somewhere.

Mary appears with an officer of the law and Mr Dodson. She calls to Sam in an agitated voice from the edge of the ice

Mary Sam! Sam!

Sam What?

Mary Come here. There's a message for Mr Pickwick and it's very important, the man says.

Sam (*to Pickwick*) Let go, sir. It's a message for you.

Pickwick You can't leave me here, Sam!

Sam It's very important.

Pickwick I'll freeze to death!

Sam shakes Pickwick off, who careers all over the ice and finishes up falling into a skater's arms. The music changes to quick tempo and quickens through the rest of the scene. Sam runs to Mary

Dodson Hand this to Mr Pickwick, if you please.

Sam A writ. (*He reads aloud.*) "Messrs Dodson and Fogg are instructed to—" 'Ere, 'ere, sir!

The Fat Boy appears and runs up on the bridge

Joe (*gasping*) Master, they ha' gone, Master, they've gone right clean off.

Wardle (*warming his hands by a brazier*) Who's gone?

Joe Mas'r Jingle and Miss Rachel, they've gone in a po'chay, to the *Blue Lion*, at Eatanswill. I was there, but I couldn't stop 'em.

Wardle Why not?

Pandemonium. Everyone is trying to get off the ice. Sam reaches Pickwick

Sam Sir, sir, look at this! (*Yelling above the hubbub*) It's a writ, sir. Messrs Dodson and Fogg are instructed by Mrs Bardell to commence an action for breach of promise against you!

The ice cracks under the strain and Pickwick disappears through it

CURTAIN

Music 11B. Entr'acte

ACT II

SCENE 1

The Town Square at Eatanswill

The set includes the inn the **Blue Lion** *and also an area reserved for the room that Jingle and Rachel have taken, preferably an upstairs room. The square is used during the musical number for parades of banners and brass bands, and for speeches made from electioneering platforms*

The Company is on stage

Music 12. Song: A Hell Of An Election!

All

Eatanswill is on the map this morning—
Free men's hopes are firmly fixed on us!
Boxing Day's a handy date
On which to choose a candidate
And we will do so with the maximum fuss.

There'll be a Hell of an Election!
In the air a smell of an election—
It'll be a difficult selection
Knowing who to choose.
We'll have a difficult decision—
We'll have to make it with precision—
For if we make the wrong decision
With the man we choose,
In the long run, we're the ones who lose!

Fizkinites

Vote for Fizkin!
Vote for Fizkin!
Horace Fizkin is too rich to work at all!

Slumkeyites

Cheats in business—
Keeps a mistress—
Always drunk at the Kent Hunt Ball.

All	Eatanswill will show the way this morning—
	We'll make sure the better man gets in!
	Slumkey may depend on his kin—
	Fizkin's wife will vote for Fizkin—
	One thing's certain—someone's going to win!
	There'll be a Hell of an Election!
	In the air a smell of an election—
	It'll be a difficult selection
	Knowing who to choose.
	We'll have a difficult decision—
	We'll have to make it with precision—
	For if we make the wrong decision
	With the man we choose,
	In the long run, we're the ones who lose!

Slumkeyites	Vote for Slumkey!
Fizkinites	Vote for Fizkin!
Slumkeyites	Vote for Slumkey!
Fizkinites	Vote for Fizkin!

The two factions start to fight

Pickwick and his party—Tupman, Snodgrass and Wardle—enter during the song and get knocked down in the battle

Slumkeyites	Vote for Slumkey!
Fizkinites	Fizkin!
Slumkeyites	Slumkey!
Fizkinites	Fizkin!
Slumkeyites	Slumkey!
Fizkinites	Vote for Fizkin!
Slumkeyites	Vote for Slumkey!
Fizkinites	Vote for Fizkin!
Slumkeyites	Vote for Slumkey!
Fizkinites	Vote for Fizkin—he's the man we choose!
Slumkeyites	Slumkey—he's the man we choose!
All	In the long run, we're the ones who lose!
	Hurrah! etc.
	Slumkey for ever! etc.

Pickwick Slumkey for ever!
Tupman Who's Slumkey?
Pickwick I've got no idea. On these occasions do what the mob does.
Snodgrass But suppose there are two mobs?
Pickwick In that case, shout for the largest. That's democracy, Tuppy.
Slumkey for ever!

Snodgrass Mr Pickwick. Have you noticed how much you resemble one of
the candidates?
Pickwick All true Blue Englishmen look alike, sir. Slumkey for ever!

Sam and Mary enter from the Blue Lion

Sam Sir. Sir, Mr Pickwick.
Mary Mr Pickwick, stop.
Pickwick Sam, what is it?
Wardle Come, man, spit it out.
Sam Well, we've been to the *Blue Lion.*
Wardle Yes, and are they there?
Sam Well, I looked outside all the rooms.
Wardle And?
Sam Well, there's a wooden leg in number six, there's a pair of hessians in
thirteen, there's two pairs of halves in the commercial, there's these here
painted tops in the snuggery inside the bar, and five more pairs of tops
in the coffee room.
Wardle Nothing more?
Sam Yes, there's a pair of Wellingtons a good deal worn and a pair of
ladies' shoes in number five.
Wardle What sort of shoes?
Sam Country make.
Wardle Any maker's name?
Sam Brown.
Wardle Where of?
Sam Muggleton.
Wardle It's them, by heavens! We've found them!
Sam The Wellingtons have been to Doctors Commons for a marriage
Licence.
Wardle I hope we are in time. Come, Sam, show us the place. Not a moment
to be lost.
Pickwick Don't be hasty, Wardle. I'd better go and help. (*To Snodgrass*)
You stay and look after Tuppy. Wardle.

*Pickwick, Sam, Wardle and Mary run right around the square and end up in
front of the* Blue Lion

Sam This is the place, sir. Here's the place.

The Landlord comes out of the inn

(*To Landlord*) Step aside.
Landlord You can't come in here.
Wardle Can't come in—why not?
Landlord We are full up, sir. Are the gentlemen Blue, sir? You see we have
the Honourable Samuel Slumkey, the parliamentary candidate, staying
here.
Pickwick Is he Blue?

Landlord Yes, he is Blue.
Pickwick Then we're Blue. Out of the way, man.

Pickwick, Wardle, Sam and Mary climb the stairs, followed by the Landlord

Is this the room?
Sam Yes, sir.
Pickwick This is the room, Wardle.
Wardle Well, in we go, Pickwick.
Pickwick Steady on. Diplomatically, Wardle.

Pickwick and Wardle enter the room. Rachel sees them and screams

You're a nice rascal, aren't you?
Pickwick Caution, sir, caution. Action for damages. Defamation of character.
Wardle How dare you drag my sister from my house?
Pickwick Well said, well said—you may well ask that—how dare, sir. How dare?
Jingle (*menacingly*) Are you talking to me?
Pickwick How, how—How do you do? He's tall (*To Sam and Mary*)—he's huge.
Wardle Pickwick, I'll have this fellow prosecuted—indicted—I'll ruin him. And you, Rachel, at a time of life when you ought to know better, what do you mean by running away with a vagabond, disgracing your family, and making yourself miserable? Get on your bonnet and come home. (*To Sam*) Call a hackney coach there, directly—(*to Landlord*)—and bring this lady's bill. D'ye hear—d'ye hear?
Sam Yes, sir.
Wardle Get on your bonnet.
Jingle Do nothing of the kind. Leave the room, sir—no business here—lady's free to act as she pleases—more than one and twenty.
Wardle More than one and twenty? More than one and forty!
Rachel I ain't!
Wardle You are! You're fifty if you're an hour!

Rachel faints into Jingle's arms

Pickwick Fetch a glass of water.
Wardle A glass of water! Bring a bucket of water and throw it all over her! It'll do her good, and she richly deserves it. Come, Pickwick, I'll carry her downstairs.
Jingle You'll do nothing of the kind, sir. Get me an officer.
Pickwick Pray consider, sir; consider.
Jingle I'll not consider, sir. This lady's her own mistress—see who dares to take her away—unless she so wishes it.
Rachel I won't be taken away. I don't wish it.
Pickwick We're in a very awkward situation, Wardle. We have no control

over this lady's actions. I warned you before we came the most we can
look for is a compromise. Leave it to me. Mr Jingle, sir; would you mind
stepping downstairs for a moment? Down the stairs.

Jingle, Pickwick and Wardle descend the stairs

Now then, my dear sir, between you and me we know that you have only
run off with this lady for the sake of her money.
Jingle How dare you say a thing like that, sir!
Pickwick Don't expostulate, sir. I say between you and me we know. We
are both men of the world and we know. Now then, my dear sir, don't
you think that fifty pounds and liberty would be better than Miss Wardle
and expectations?
Jingle No!
Pickwick Eh! Seventy? Eighty? Well, what then?
Jingle Won't do, sir.
Pickwick Damn it, sir; just tell me what will do.
Jingle Expensive affair, money out of pocket—let's see now....

music   **Music 13. Song: Very**

Posting nine pounds, licence four pounds—
Compensation many more pounds—
Breach of honour, loss of lady, hard to bury.
Have no wish to be offensive,
But feel slightly apprehensive
That the recompense will prove expensive—very.
Pickwick (*speaking*) Jingle, how can you be such a villain, sir?
Jingle (*speaking*) Simple matter, very.
(*Singing*) Life's a challenge, can't deny it—
Always try to profit by it.
My philosophy of life is short but merry.
It's a toy for us to play with—
Like a dream you spend the day with—
And there's little you can't get away with—very.
Wardle (*speaking*) Beats me how the devil you persuade these foolish women
to listen to you.
Jingle (*speaking*) My dear sir.
(*Singing*) If a lady needs persuasion,
There's a rule for each occasion—
One adopts whichever one is necessary.
If she's childish, give her candy—
If she's nervous, give her brandy—
If she's easy, well, of course, that's handy—very.
Pickwick (*speaking*) Say a hundred, sir?
Jingle (*speaking*) And twenty?
Pickwick (*speaking*) My dear sir—

Wardle (*speaking*) Oh, let's give it to him and let him go.
Jingle   (*singing*) Pray don't think me bold or brash, sir—
                          'Fraid I must insist on cash, sir,
                          For to me a sovereign's not unlike a cherry—
                          Why take one when there are plenty—
                          Take a hundred, sir, and twenty—
                          And be on your way, subitamente—very!
(*Speaking*) Here's the wedding licence, get the name altered, do for
Tuppy.
                          (*Singing*) I'm a hell of a devil on every level. . . .
Pickwick   And a bit of a character, too!

Jingle exits

Wardle Come on home, Rachel.

*Pickwick and Wardle collect Rachel after Jingle's exit and emerge from the
inn. A crowd of people have collected outside the inn during the scene. As
Pickwick emerges the Pickwickians rush up to congratulate him on his
victory. His good mood prompts him to pat a nearby child on the head. The
crowd, mistaking him for the candidate, chair him around the square whilst
he and the Pickwickians protest to no avail*

Cheer Leader There's Samuel Slumkey! He's come out!
Crowd Hurrah!
Cheer Leader He's shaking hands with all the men.
Crowd Hurrah!
Cheer leader He's patting the babies on the head.
Crowd Hurrah!
Cheer Leader He's *kissed* one of them! He's kissing them *all*!
Crowd Hurrah!

Music 13A. Hell Of An Election (*orchestral reprise*)   **music**

*During Music 13A there is much bustling amongst the crowd and Pickwick
appears on top of a truck with the Town Crier*

We want Slumkey! We want Slumkey! Speech, speech, etc.!
Pickwick Please, you've made a terrible mistake. I'm not Slumkey. My
name's Pickwick, Samuel Pickwick—you've got the wrong fellow. You
might regret it.

music   **Music 14. Song: If I Ruled The World**

    (*Singing*)   Friends; dear friends,
May I say I'm not a politician!—
A single-minded, silver-tongued magician—
Whose words, fine words,
Could charm the very birds
From the trees. . . .   *Cheers*
With ease.   *More Cheers*

Please, dear friends,
Though I may not be the world's physician—
By nature I'm of modest disposition—
Suppose, you chose,
Instead of men like those,
Men like these!   *Cheers*
And these!   *More Cheers*

Men who want a world that's fine and free.
Men like Nelson, Wellington and Drake and me.
We want a world our children will be proud to see.
And if I had the chance,
I know just how it would be.

If I ruled the world,
Every day would be the first day of Spring—
Every heart would have a new song to sing—
And we'd sing
Of the joy every morning would bring.

If I ruled the world,
Every man would be as free as a bird—
Every voice would be a voice to be heard—
Take my word,
We would treasure each day that occurred.

My world
Would be a beautiful place,
Where we would weave such wonderful dreams.
My world
Would wear a smile on its face—
Like the man in the moon has when the moon beams.

If I ruled the world,
Every man would say the world was his friend.
There'd be happiness that no man could end—

No, my friend,
Not if I ruled the world.

Every head would be held up high—
There'd be sunshine in everyone's sky—
If the day ever dawned when I
Ruled the world.

The scene changes to the legal offices of Dodson and Fogg. Pickwick is kept in focus as he sings on top of one of the towers and the company sing as the towers are moved to the new setting

All   Our world
                    Would be a beautiful place
                    Where we would weave such wonderful dreams.
                    Our world
                    Would wear a smile on its face
                    Like the man in the moon has when the moon beams.

                    If he ruled the world,
                    Every man would say the world was his friend—
                    There'd be happiness that no man could end—
                    No, my friend,
                    Not if he ruled the world.
                    Every head would be held up high—
                    There'd be sunshine in everyone's sky—
                    If the day ever dawned when he
                    Ruled the world.

SCENE 2

The Office of Dodson and Fogg

Inside the office are Dodson, Fogg, the Clerk—Mr Jackson—and a second clerk

Tony Weller and Sam meet outside the office

Tony Sammy!
Sam Me ancient, me old codger.
Tony Yes it is, Samivel.
Sam How are you, my ancient?
Tony Why, Sammy, I haven't seen you for two years and better.

Sam No more you have, old codger. How's Mrs Weller?

Tony I'll tell you what, Sammy. As a widder there never was a nicer woman than that there second wentur o' mine—a sweet creature she was, Sammy; and as she was such an uncommon pleasant widder, it's a great pity she ever changed her condition. She didn't never act as a wife, Sammy.

Sam Didn't she though?

Tony No, I've done it once too often, Sammy, I've done it once too often. Take example by your father, my boy, and be very careful of widders all your life, especially if they've kept a public house, Sammy.

Sam Righto, then, I will, but how is she nonetheless?

Tony Dead and done for, Sammy, dead and done for. Regret over marrying beneath her took her off. You're an orphan agin, Sammy.

Sam Oh, well, cheer up then, old un, you're on the loose agin, aren't you?

Tony What's the use, Sammy, I'm in for the high jump. Sooner nor later some widder will cop me. What brings you to the eye of the law—women? The curse of the Vellers, Sammy, the curse of the Vellers. Be a better father than I have, Sam, stay a bachelor all your life.

music   **Music 15. Song: The Trouble With Women**

(*Singing*)   Life can be a treacherous sea
                       For men such as we to swim in—
                       Infested as it always is
                       With bachelor-eating women.

                       Men are a mixture of sweetness and kindness—
                       We're generous and infinitely charming.
                       Our minds are strong and active—
                       We're very attractive—
                       And women, quite naturally,
                       Find us utterly disarming.

Tony⎫ (*together*) That's the trouble with women—
Sam ⎭   They don't give men a chance!
                       They trap a feller nine times out of ten.
                       Yes, that's the trouble with women—
                       And men should ignore them—
                       But they don't!—
                       And that's the trouble with men!

Sam   Women are a mixture of shrewdness and cunning—
                       So credible not many men suspect them.
                       Their minds are weak and pliable—
                       They're none too reliable—
                       And some men, quite naturally,
                       Feel they really must protect them.

Tony ⎱ *(together)* **Sam** ⎰	That's the trouble with women— They grab all they can get! If only they would learn when to say when. There'd be no trouble with women If men did without them— But they can't!— And that's the trouble with men!
Tony **Sam** **Tony** **Sam** **Tony** ⎱ *(together)* **Sam** ⎰	Men are a mixture of virtue and loyalty— We need no other label to assist us. We're modest and we're truthful— Perennially youthful— And women, quite naturally, Are unable to resist us.
	That's the trouble with women— They won't leave men alone! I've seen it happen time and time again. You know the trouble with women— They think they can fool us— And they can!— And that's the trouble with men!
Sam **Tony** **Tony** ⎱ *(together)* **Sam** ⎰	Women are a mixture of meanness and cruelty— I sometimes wonder why men don't despise them! They bicker and quarrel— They're vain and immoral— And some men, quite naturally, Try to comfort and advise them.
Tony **Sam** ⎱ *(together)* **Tony** ⎰	That's the trouble with women— They simply won't let go! They'll hang on till the parson says Amen! Yes, that's the trouble with women— They want to get married— And they do!— And that's the trouble— It's there you'll find the trouble— With men! Oh yes!— It's there you'll find the trouble with men!

Pickwick enters with the Pickwickians

Pickwick My name is Samuel Pickwick. I have an appointment with Messrs Dodson and Fogg—ah, Sam.

Sam This is my gentleman, ancient, Mr Pickwick, my dad—to the best of my knowledge.

Pickwick A very good choice on both sides.

Tony I hope you haven't got no fault to find with Sammy, sir. I took a great deal of pains with his education. I let him run in the streets when he was very young and shift for himself. And if you want my advice you'll come away from here, Battledore and Shuttlecock's a wery good game if you ain't the shuttlecock and them two lawyers the battledores.
Clerk This way, Mr Pickwick. This is Mr Pickwick, sir.

Pickwick is ushered into the office of Dodson and Fogg who sit perched on high stools above Pickwick's head. Dodson is a very tall, thin gentleman and Fogg a tiny one

Dodson Ah. You are the defendant, sir, in Bardell and Pickwick.
Fogg An action for Breach of Promise of Marriage.
Pickwick I am, sir.
Dodson And what do you propose?
Fogg Yes, sir. What do you propose?
Pickwick What grounds of action do you have against me, gentlemen?
Dodson Actions?
Dodson Grounds?
Dodson Consult your own conscience, sir.
Fogg Consult it, sir.
Dodson We are guided by the statement of our client.
Fogg Mrs Bardell, our client.
Dodson That statement, sir, may be true.
Fogg It may be true.
Dodson It may be false.
Fogg It may be false.
Dodson It may be credible.
Fogg It may be incredible.
Dodson But if it be true—
Fogg And if it be credible—
Dodson What do you mean "if it be credible?"
Fogg If it not be incredible—
Dodson Two negatives make proof positive, Mr Fogg.
Fogg Your case is unanswerable, Mr Dodson.
Dodson You may be a very unfortunate man, sir.
Fogg Unfortunate.
Dodson Or you may be a designing one.
Fogg Designing.
Dodson I personally could come to but one verdict.
Pickwick And what is that verdict?
Dodson ⎱ (*together*) Guilty—Damages fifteen hundred pounds.
Fogg ⎰
Pickwick Of all the disgraceful and rascally proceedings!
Dodson Stay, sir, stay—Mr Jackson.
Clerk Sir.
Dodson Hear what this gentleman has to say.
Clerks Sir.

Dodson Mr Wicks.

2nd Clerk Sir.

Dodson Pray continue, sir.

Fogg Yes, continue, sir.

Dodson Disgraceful and rascally proceedings, I think you said, sir.

Pickwick I did. I said, sir, that of all the disgraceful and rascally proceedings that were ever attempted, this is the most so. I repeat it, sir.

Sam No, sir, no.

Dodson You hear that, Wicks?

2nd Clerk Oh yes, sir.

Fogg You won't forget these expressions, Mr Jackson?

Clerk Oh, no, sir.

Dodson Perhaps you would like to call us swindlers, sir. Pray do so, if you feel so disposed.

Tupman No please, Pickwick, no.

Pickwick I *will*. You *are* swindlers!

Winkle Oh no!

Snodgrass Oh, Lord!

Dodson Very good. You can hear, I hope, Mr Wicks.

2nd Clerk Oh yes, sir.

Fogg You had better come a little closer, Wicks.

2nd clerk Yes, sir.

Fogg You too, Jackson.

Clerk Yes, sir.

Dodson Do go on, sir, do go on. You had better call us thieves, sir.

Snodgrass Don't do it, sir.

Pickwick I will, I will!

Fogg Perhaps you would like to assault one of us.

Pickwick I would, yes, indeed I would!

Sam No, sir, no! They'll have you for every last farthing.

Dodson We will not make the smallest resistance. We like to be insulted, don't we, Mr Fogg?

Fogg It's a pleasure, Mr Dodson.

Dodson It's an income, Mr Fogg.

Music 16. Song: That's The Law!   music

Dodson⎫
Fogg ⎭
That's the law! That's the law!
It's a highly legal business is the law.
Never try to get the better of the law.
You'll be the debtor of the law.
And that's the letter of the law!

Lawyers
We are highly independent.
If we act for the defendant,
We make sure before the case we cannot lose it.

Pickwickians	But if they detect a faint 'if They switch over to the plaintiff. They have got a lot of influence—
Dodson } **Fogg**	And we use it!
Lawyers **Pickwickians** **Lawyers** **Pickwickians** **All**	That's the law! That's the law! That's the law! That's the law! They are rich because they represent the poor! Never try to get the better—of the law— You'll be the debtor—of the law— And that's the letter of the law!
Lawyers **Pickwickians**	Take the case of Rex v. Drury— Mr Drury owned a brewery— He was charged with things he openly admitted. They took members of the jury On a visit to the brewery— And the next day Mr Drury was acquitted!
Lawyers **Pickwickians** **Lawyers** **Pickwickians** **Dodson** } **Fogg** **All**	That's the law! That's the law! That's the law! That's the law! Oh, it pays to be a shrewd solicitor! That's the law! Never try to get the better—of the law— You'll be the debtor—of the law— And that's the letter of the law!
Pickwickians **Dodson** } **Fogg** **Pickwickians** **Lawyers** **Pickwickians** **Lawyers** **Dodson** } **Fogg** **All**	City banker name of Thunder Made a monumental blunder— Little wonder he could see the trouble mounting. He'd embezzled fifty thousand— Built himself a nifty house and It's as well for him that we did his accounting! That's the law! That's the law! That's the law! That's the law! Now he's richer than he ever was before! That's the law! Never try to get the better of the law.

You'll be the debtor—of the law.
And that's the letter of the law!

Lawyers   Like that lady Prudence Presser—
                 Shot her husband, a professor—
Pickwickians When she found him entertaining several students.
                 But a promise to the poor man
Lawyers   Who was picked as jury foreman
Pickwickians Won the verdict—
All   —What you might call
                 "Jury's Prudence."!

Pickwickians That's the law!
Lawyers   That's the law!
Pickwickians That's the law!
Lawyers   That's the law!
                 And our clients include three bishops and a whore!

The set starts to change here. The Courtroom ought to be the largest scene in the show. The main body of the court faces the audience presuming the judge to be high in the upper circle and the jury in the auditorium

All   That's the law!
                 Never try to get the better—of the law.
                 You'll be the debtor—of the law.
                 And that's the letter of the law.

                 That's the law! That's the law!
                 That's the law! That's the law!
                 Oh, it pays to be a shrewd solicitor!
                 Never try to get the better—of the law.
                 You'll be the debtor—of the law.
                 And that's the letter of the law!

SCENE 3

The Courtroom

The Company are on stage including Sergeant Buzfuz, Mr Skimpkin, Sergeant Snubbins and Mr Funky

The Usher bangs his stave three times

Voice Silence in the court!
Officer Bardell v Pickwick.
Buzfuz I am for the plaintiff, my Lord.

The Judge's voice comes from as high up in the circle as it can be. He is old and deaf and unintelligent

Judge Who is with you, brother Buzfuz?
Buzfuz Mr Skimpkin, my Lord.

Skimpkin bows to intimate that he is

Snubbins I appear for the defendant, my Lord.
Judge Anyone with you, Snubbins?
Snubbins Mr Funky, my Lord.
Judge Sergeant Buzfuz and Mr Skimpkin for the plaintiff. For the defendant—Sergeant Snubbins and Mr Monkey.
Snubbins Beg your Lordship's pardon—Funky.
Judge (*testily*) I *said* Monkey! You may proceed, Sergeant Buzfuz.

Buzfuz is an accomplished and very dramatic orator

Buzfuz Gentlemen, you have heard that this is an action for a breach of promise of marriage, in which the damages are laid at fifteen hundred pounds. The plaintiff, who I am about to place in that box, is an unimpeachable female. She is, gentlemen, a widow. The late Mr Bardell, after enjoying for many years the esteem and confidence of his sovereign—he was a Customs Officer, one of the guardians of the Royal Revenues— glided almost imperceptibly from the world, to seek elsewhere for that repose and peace which a Custom House can never afford. (*He falters, overcome by emotion*) Some time before his death he had stamped his likeness upon a little boy. With this little boy, the only pledge of her departed exciseman, Mrs Bardell took up the challenging gauntlet the hard world throws down before widowed ladies with young to raise and care for, and took up the onerous duties of Manageress of what had been and remained until the advent of a certain party, a decent hostelry. Here she placed in the front saloon window a written placard, bearing this inscription—"Chambers furnished for single gentleman. Enquire within".
Judge There is no date to that, is there, Sergeant Buzfuz?
Buzfuz There is no date, my Lord, but I entreat the attention of the Jury to the wording of this document—"Chambers furnished for single Gentleman"! Mrs Bardell's opinions of the opposite sex, gentlemen, were derived from a long contemplation of the inestimable qualities of her lost husband. She had no fear—she had no distrust—she had no suspicion— all was confidence and reliance. "Mr Bardell," said the widow, "Mr Bardell was a man of honour—Mr Bardell was a man of his word—Mr Bardell was no deceiver—Mr Bardell was once a single gentleman himself: to single gentlemen I look for protection, for assistance, for comfort, and for consolation—in single gentlemen I shall perpetually see something to remind me of what Mr Bardell was, when he first won my young and untried affections; by single gentlemen, then, shall my chambers be filled." Actuated by this beautiful and touching impulse, among the best impulses

of our imperfect nature, gentlemen, the lonely and desolate widow dried her tears, furnished her chambers, caught her innocent boy to her maternal bosom and put the bill up in her saloon window. Did it remain there long? No. The serpent was on the watch.

Mrs Bardell bursts into tears and is helped back to her seat

Within three days—three days, gentlemen—a being, erect upon two legs, and bearing all the outward semblance of a man, and not of a monster, called loudly at the ever open doors of the *George and Vulture*. He enquired within; he took the chambers; and on the very next day entered into possession of them. This man was Pickwick—Pickwick the defendant.

Pickwick is placed in the box

Of this man Pickwick I will say little; the subject presents but a few attractions, and I, gentlemen, am not the man, nor are you, gentlemen, the men, to delight in the contemplation of revolting heartlessness, and of systematic villainy. I say systematic villainy, gentlemen, and when I say systematic villainy, let me tell the defendant, Pickwick, it would have been more decent in him, more becoming, in better judgment and in better taste, if he had never set foot in this Court. Let me tell him, gentlemen, that any gestures of dissent or disapprobation in which he may indulge in this Court will not go down with you; that you will know how to value and how to appreciate them; and let me tell him further, as my Lord will tell you, gentlemen, that a counsel, in the discharge of his duty to his client, is neither to be intimidated nor bullied, nor put down; and that any attempt to do either the one or the other or the first, or the last, will recoil on the head of the attempter, be he plaintiff or be he defendant, be his name Pickwick or Noakes, or Stoakes, or Stiles, or Brown or Thompson.

This produces the intended effect of turning all eyes on Pickwick

I am in a situation to prove to you, gentlemen, on the testimony of three of his own friends—most unwilling witnesses, gentlemen, most unwilling witnesses, that on that morning he was discovered by them on a bed, holding the plaintiff in his arms and smothering her with his caresses and endearments. And now, gentlemen, but one word more. Two letters have passed between these parties; letters which are admitted to be in the handwriting of the defendant and which speak volumes indeed. Letters intended at that time, by Pickwick, to mislead and delude any third party into whose hands they might fall. They are not open, fervent, eloquent epistles, breathing nothing but the language of affectionate attachment. They are covert, sly, underhanded communications, BUT fortunately far more conclusive than if couched in the most glowing language and the most poetic imagery. Let me read the first to you—"Dear Mrs B, I shall not be home until to-morrow. Slow Coach"—then follows a most remarkable expression—"Don't trouble yourself about the warming pan". Now let me read the second letter to you—"Dear Mrs B. Chops and Tomato Sauce, Yours Pickwick". Chops! Gracious heavens and tomato sauce! Gentlemen, is the happiness of a sensitive and confiding female to be trifled away by such shallow artifices as these?

Crowd No, no!

Usher Silence in the Court.

Buzfuz Enough, gentlemen, enough; my client's hopes and prospects are ruined and it is no figure of speech to say that the heart has gone out of her. The voice of the little boy is hushed, his infant sports disregarded when his mother weeps. But Pickwick, gentlemen, Pickwick, the ruthless destroyer of this domestic hostelry in the desert of South Rochester—Pickwick, who has choked up the well and thrown ashes on the sward—Pickwick who comes before you to-day with his heartless tomato sauce, his absent warming pans, and his boneless chops! Pickwick, still rears his ugly head and unblushing effrontery and gazes without a sigh upon the ruin he has made. Damages, gentlemen, heavy damages, is the only punishment with which you can visit him; and the only recompense you can award to my client. And for those damages, she now appeals to you, the jury; to an enlightened, a high-minded, a right-feeling, a conscientious, a dispassionate, a sympathising, a contemplative jury of her civilised countrymen. That concludes the case for the plaintiff, my lord.

Snubbins For the defence, my lord—

Judge In summing up this scandalous case, I feel it is my duty to point out to the jury that if Mrs Bardell is right, then, er—Mr Pickwick is wrong; and if you believe the evidence you have heard, why then you'll believe it, and if you don't, why then you won't; and that, gentlemen of the jury, is my personal opinion of this dreadful man Pickwick.

music **Snubbins** For the defence, my lord—

Usher Gentlemen, are you all agreed upon your verdict?

Foreman Yes, we are.

Usher Do you find for the plaintiff, gentlemen, or for the defendant?

Foreman For the plaintiff.

Usher With what damages?

Foreman Seven hundred and fifty pounds.

Pickwick I will NOT pay!

music   **Music 17. Song: British Justice**

Throughout the number Pickwick counter-sings "I WILL NOT PAY"

During the number the Pickwickians, Dodson and Fogg, Sam, Mrs Bardell, Bardell Jnr, Rachel, Isabella and Emily are DS

All   British Justice!
                               Rah, rah, rah!

Jolly good show!
Hear, hear, hear!
It's tophole and simply splendid,
Don't you know!
Hear, hear, hear, hear!

Pickwick   British justice has prevailed—
Innocent men are often jailed—
But the system's never failed—

All   Oh, jolly good show!
Hear, hear, hear, hear!

All   Pip, pip, tally ho!
Chin, chin, cheerio!
Three cheers! Hip, hip, hurray!
For jolly old British justice
Is jolly well here to stay.

All   Good show, good show!
Oh, jolly good show!
What a jolly, jolly, good show!
There's nothing quite so jolly, you know,
As a jolly, jolly, good show!

Pickwick   May I be allowed to say,
I've just decided not to pay.

All   British Empire—
Pickwick   Oh, God bless her!
All   Jolly good show!
Hear, hear, hear!
It's the marvel of the ages,
Don't you know!
Hear, hear, hear, hear!
Pickwick   It is run by thieves and fools—
But they've all been to public schools—
So Britannia waives the rules!
All   Oh, jolly good show!
Hear, hear, hear, hear!

*The setting begins to change here to the Fleet Prison and the number of
choruses is only conditioned by how long the change of setting takes to
complete*

Pip, pip, tally ho!
Chin, chin, cheerio!
Three cheers, hip, hip, hurray!

<table>
<tr><td></td><td>For jolly old British Empire
Is jolly well here to stay.</td></tr>
<tr><td>All</td><td>Good show, good show!
Oh jolly good show!
What a jolly, jolly, jolly good show!
There's nothing quite so jolly, you know,
As a jolly, jolly good show!</td></tr>
<tr><td></td><td>Pip, pip, tally ho!
Chin, chin, cheerio!
Three cheers! Hip, hip, hurray!</td></tr>
<tr><td></td><td>For jolly old British Empire
Is jolly well here to stay!
Good show, good show!
Oh, jolly good show!
What a jolly, jolly good show!
There's nothing quite so jolly you know,
As a jolly, jolly good show!</td></tr>
<tr><td>Pickwick</td><td>I will NOT pay.</td></tr>
</table>

On Pickwick's last line, the line of people divides and they march off each side

SCENE 4

Inside the Fleet Prison

This is where, as the flashback is completed, the courtroom crowd put on their debtors' rags in front of the audience. Again it is done fairly deliberately and certainly not in a rush. Pickwick is found with Sam in exactly the position he began and the prison setting is of course identical

Pickwick   Christmas Eve at the *George and Vulture*. . . .
                      That's where it all began, Sam—
                      That's where it all began.

Voices offstage sing:

Turnkey	Business is booming. . . .
Hot Toddy Man	Hot Whisky Toddy. . . .
Cold Drinks Man	Good for your liver. . . .
Turnkey	Business is booming. . . .
Hot Toddy Man	Hot Whisky Toddy. . . .

Cold Drinks Man   Good for your liver....
Jingle (*as a debtor*) Help the poor debtors ...
                          Help the poor debtors ...
Sam Mr Pickwick, sir—it's Mr Jingle.
Pickwick Bless my soul—so it is—give me your hand.
Jingle No indeed, rather not.
Pickwick Nonsense, come along, lean on me.
Jingle Thank you. Not too fast—legs shaky—head queer—round and round—earthquaky sort of feeling—very.
Pickwick What are you doing here?
Jingle Unfortunate business—paltry debts—most embarrassing—very.
Pickwick Sit down, sir.
Jingle Oh, thank you.
Pickwick Let me pour you some wine. (*He takes a bottle and a glass out of a hamper*)
Jingle Oh, no, sir, no, couldn't get it down, sir. Lived on a pair of boots—whole fortnight. Silk umbrella—ivory handle—a week.
Pickwick Ate them?
Jingle Pawned them.
Pickwick Come along, sir, drink this.
Jingle No, sir, choke me.
Pickwick Weak stomach?
Jingle Strong conscience. Mr Pickwick, sir, I haven't led a blameless life, not exactly—ungrateful dog—boyish to cry—can't help it—suffered much.
Pickwick Try a chop.
Jingle No, don't deserve it, sir.
Pickwick Damn it, sir, if we all got what we deserved, we'd all be in the Fleet for the rest of our lives.
Jingle You've convinced me, sir.
Pickwick Take the cheese?
Jingle Try the chop.
Pickwick Take them both.

There is shouting off stage

Pickwick What's all that noise going on? Can't we have some peace and quiet in the prison?
Sam Sir, it's Mrs Bardell!
Mob Mrs Bardell, Mrs Bardell.

Mrs Bardell enters with her son

It's Mrs Bardell herself.
George It's that nasty old man again.
Mrs Bardell Oh! Mr Pickwick, sir, how can you ever forgive me, sir?
Pickwick What are you doing here, Mrs Bardell?
Mrs Bardell I'm telling you one and all that I've been fell upon and cast in

here for not paying my debts to them Dodson and Fogg pair. Perish the day I ever listened to their serpents' tongues.

Pickwick For debt? Explain yourself, Madam.

Mrs Bardell I shall do that, sir. I was sitting quietly in my parlour thinking of the good old days, sir, when I used to bring up your breakfast, sir, having prepared it with my own hands, sir.

Pickwick Yes, yes, we know what all *that* led to!

Mrs Bardell Oh! I'm so contrite, sir.

Pickwick And what happened then?

Mrs Bardell Up comes a couple of constables and before I could so much as pack a spare shift, they had me in here for not paying my legal debts to that pair to whose name I wouldn't sink so low as to soil my lips with, Dodson and Fogg.

Pickwick Mrs Bardell, I feel myself responsible for your present condition.

Mrs Bardell Condition? I may be poor, Mr Pickwick, but I am untouched by dishonour.

Pickwick Mrs Bardell, I mean your incarceration in this place, madam. I feel myself personally responsible for it.

Sam Wait a minute, sir.

Pickwick If I had paid my damages, this poor innocent widow lady—

Sam Innocent? Her! She got you in here in the first place, didn't she?

Pickwick Don't interrupt the train of my logic, Sam. If, as I say, I had paid my damages, this poor innocent widow lady and her brat—

Mrs Bardell Brat!

Pickwick Brat, madam.

Mrs Bardell You're right—he *is* a brat! (*She cuffs Georgie*)

Pickwick Mrs Bardell!

Mrs Bardell Yes, sir. I do think as how two can live as cheaply as one—

Pickwick No, no, Mrs Bardell—what I wish to say is—

Mrs Bardell Oh, yes, sir—granted before ever asked.

Pickwick Please, Mrs Bardell—

Mrs Bardell Oh, no, sir, the pleasure is entirely mine.

Pickwick (*violently*) Silence, woman!

Mrs Bardell Oh, sir! 'Ow thrilling! I never knew you had a violent side to you.

Pickwick (*pleadingly*) Please, Mrs Bardell, be quiet for a moment.

Mrs Bardell Whatever you wish, sir. Quiet or noisy, ever at your service, yours sincerely, Mrs Bardell.

Pickwick Mrs Bardell, I wish to make amends to you. I intend to pay your paltry debts.

Mrs Bardell Why ever should you, Mr Pickwick?

Jingle Don't stop him, marm. Rare mood. Cultivate it. You're quite right, Mr Pickwick, sir. Quite right.

Pickwick On second thoughts I shall pay your paltry debts too, Jingle.

Jingle You see, madam.

Music 18. Song: Do As You Would Be Done By   music

(*Singing*)
Do as you would be done by—
Practise what you preach!
Give away anything—
But promises
You must keep.

Pickwick
Sam
Mrs Bardell
Jingle
Do unto others
As you would have others
Do unto you.
Do as you would be done by—
And others will, too!

Pickwick
Take a man like me—
Enlightened, creative—
With many kinds of talent
That are best described as native.
I'm a part-time philosopher—
As any man can be—
And this is part of my philosophy.

Pickwick
Sam
Mrs Bardell
Jingle
Do as you would be done by—
Sow as you would reap!
Give away anything—
But promises
You must keep.

All
Do unto others
As you would have others
Do unto you.

Do as you would be done by—
And others will, too!

Sam
Take a bloke like me—
Resourceful, inventive—
There's nothing I won't do
If I'm given the incentive.
I'll support any enterprise
That keeps me out of jail!
With these ingredients
I just can't fail.

Pickwick
Sam
Mrs Bardell
Jingle
Do as you would be done by—
Sow as you would reap.
Give away anything—
But promises
You must keep.

All   Do unto others
                   As you would have others
                   Do unto you.
                   Do as you would be done by—
                   And others will, too!

Jingle   Take a chap like me—
                   Attractive, disarming—
                   There's nothing I would do
                   That isn't absolutely charming.
                   But I'm most unreliable—
                   Some people say a fool—
                   But even I observe the golden rule!
Pickwick ⎫   Do as you would be done by—
Sam   ⎪   Give as well as take.
Mrs Bardell ⎬ Give away anything—
Jingle   ⎭   But promises
                   You can't break.

All   Do unto others
                   As you would have others
                   Do unto you.

                   Do as you would be done by—
                   And others will, too!

Mrs Bardell   Take a girl like me—
                   Protective, maternal—
                   I'm looking for a gentleman
                   Who wants to be paternal.
                   So I pamper and flatter them—
                   And give 'em cups of tea
                   And say things I would have them say to me.

All   Do as you would be done by—
                   Practise what you preach.
                   Give away anything—
                   But promises
                   You can't breach!

                   Do unto others
                   As you would have others
                   Do unto you.

	Do as you would be done by
	And others will, too!
Coda	And others will—
	Yes, others will!
	Your fathers and your mothers
	And your sisters and your brothers
	And a hundred thousand others
	Will, too!

A hunting horn is heard off stage

Pickwick   That's Winkle! I'd know that note anywhere.
Voices   Turnkey—open the gates—tally ho!—ho there!

The three Pickwickians and the Turnkey appear at the back of the Prison

Tupman Release that gentleman.
Turnkey On what authority?
Snodgrass On this authority, sir. The authority of Dodson.
Winkle And this, the authority of Fogg.
Tupman You are free, sir!
Snodgrass Free as a bird!
Winkle Free as air!
Tupman We have sacrificed ourselves, sir.
Pickwick Sacrificed?
Snodgrass In a manner of speaking, sir, well, we have become—engaged.
Pickwick What!
Winkle Engaged to three heiresses.
Snodgrass To the three Wardle ladies.
Pickwick But what about the principles of the Club? What about the principles of the Club?
Snodgrass Damn it, sir, we did it for *you!*
Pickwick That's not the point, you thundering, blithering, blathering, bumbling nincompoops!
Winkle Thank you very much, sir.
Tupman But, sir, on the strength of our engagements—we have jointly raised the funds and purchased your release from Messrs Dodson and Fogg.

Growls from the crowd as Dodson and Fogg approach

Pickwick You mean you paid these rascals seven hundred and fifty solid golden sovereigns?

Pickwickians We did, sir.

Pickwick You've paid these double-dyed, thieving rascals their money?

Tupman Why, yes, sir.

Snodgrass That was the idea.

Winkle To save you, sir, from yourself, sir.

Pickwick But damn and blast it, gentlemen, I don't wish to be saved. I'm perfectly comfortable here.

Dodson I am afraid you have no alternative, sir.

Fogg It is illegal to remain in prison once your debts are paid.

Dodson Quite improper. Now that Mrs Bardell has received her damages—

Pickwick Ah! Yes, how is your client, gentlemen?

Dodson Oh! Very comfortable, sir.

Fogg I believe she's taken a small public house in the West Country. Is that not so, Mr Dodson?

Dodson East Anglia, Mr Fogg.

Pickwick And doubtless you gentlemen have recovered your expenses from Mrs Bardell's damages?

Dodson A mere pittance, sir.

Fogg We let the lady off lightly.

Pickwick Mrs Bardell!

Mrs Bardell (*coming forward*) At your service, sir.

Dodson You served the writ to the wrong debtor's prison, Mr Fogg. I said the Clink.

Fogg You said the Fleet, Mr Dodson.

Dodson The Clink, sir! I said the Clink!

Pickwick You understand, madam, these foolish gentlemen have paid your damages in full.

Mrs Bardell You paid them? You paid that pair?

Tupman We did, madam, every last penny.

Mrs Bardell The double-dyed, stinking, rotten, lying, thieving, conniving, cheating, widow-and orphant-robbing B-Barristers.

Pickwick Stay, stay where you are, Fogson and Dodd, Dodson and Fogg. This lady is withdrawing her charges against me. You must repay these gentlemen their—her—my money. Sam!

Dodson Mr Fogg, I think we'd better.

Fogg Mr Dodson, you're a debtor.

Pickwick I shall also settle Mr Jingle's paltry debt. I should also pay Mr Sam Weller's small account and Mrs Bardell's paltry debt.

Mob And mine, sir, and mine.

Pickwick Mr Jackson's paltry debt. Robinson, Jallop's paltry debt, etc.

Mob And mine, sir, and mine.

Music 19. Song: The Pickwickians (*reprise*)   music

*During this reprise, the scene changes to the outside of the Fleet Prison. The
debtors have dispersed; only the gate is on stage*

All
Picture if you can,
A shy, intelligent man—
Very few have an intellect as sparkling as his.
Some may doubt that his genius is great—
But it is!
Oh it is, to say the least!
And his praises we shall sing!
We are proud to be acquainted with a great, great man!
The man's a Prince! A Duke! A King!
A King!

That's Pickwick!
That's Pickwick!
Beyond a shadow of a doubt, that's Pickwick!
As civilised and splendid as a man can be—
Samuel Willoughby Pickwick—
That's he!

They were idealists, now they must scrub
The principles of freedom of the Pickwick Club!
The Pickwick Club!

Crowd
Good-bye, Mr Pickwick! Good-bye, Mr Pickwick!

SCENE 5

Outside the Fleet Prison

*The Pickwickians and Tony Weller, pass through the gate with Isabella, Emily
and Rachel and a woman debtor, saying good-bye to Pickwick in turn. Georgie
chases through the gate after Mrs Bardell*

Pickwick The Pickwick Club is dissolved, gentlemen, completely dissolved.

Music 20. Song: If I Ruled The World (*reprise*)   music

(*Singing*)
If I ruled the world,
Every man would be as free as a bird!
Every voice would be a voice to be heard—

Take my word,
We would treasure each day that occurred.

My world
Would be a beautiful place,
With every day as happy as this
My world
Would wear a smile on its face—
Like the Man in the Moon has
When the moon beams.

If I ruled the world,
Every man would say the world was his friend.
There'd be happiness that no man could end—
No, my friend,
Not if I ruled the world.
Every head would be held up high—
There'd be sunshine in everyone's sky—
If the day ever dawned
When I ruled the world!

The Turnkey escorts Sam to the gate and locks it after Sam passes through

Sam Wait for me, sir!
Pickwick Sam, I thought you'd left me too.
Sam I can't very well, sir, can I? After all, I'm your gentleman and you're my gentleman, ain't we, sir? It's like a sort of permanent engagement, as the spinster barmaid said to the septuagenarian tippler.
Pickwick Sam, don't you think we should record for posterity the activities of our famous club?
Sam Good idea, sir, wery.
Pickwick Take it down, Sam.

Sam takes a pencil and notebook out of his pocket

The posthumous papers of the Pickwick Club. The first ray of light which illumines the gloom and converts into a dazzling brilliancy the public career of—what shall I say, Sam? Mr Pickwick, Samuel Pickwick Esquire, or merely Pickwick?
Sam Say, sir, nothing less than the immortal Pickwick.

Pickwick continues the dictation as the music surges up and the CURTAIN slowly falls

Music 21. Entr'acte Music for Curtain Calls

FURNITURE AND PROPERTY LIST

Please see staging notes in the Introduction.
As each scene "melts" into the next, with the cast bringing on whichever essential properties it needs for each scene, only properties mentioned in the script are listed here.

ACT I

Scene 1

Off stage: Vendors' carts (**Vendors**)
Wheelbarrow. On it: luggage (**Sam**)

Personal: **Turnkey:** keys

Scene 2

Off stage: Bundles of "rags" (**Debtors**)
Coins in metal mugs (**Women**)
Games, cards etc (**Debtors**)
Baskets for clothes (**Debtors**)
Pickwick's bags and "comforts" including a hamper containing wine, glasses and food (**Sam and Tony**)

Personal: **Tony:** purse with money

Scene 3

Off stage: Pickwick's table and chair (**Ostler**)
Food (**Company**)
Drink (**Company**)
Stage coach. On it: luggage (**Stage Management**)

Personal: **Jingle:** brown paper parcel
Snodgrass: notebook, pencil, watch
Tupman: money

SCENE 4

Off stage: Trays of punch (**Company**)

Personal: **Tupman:** wallet containing notes
Dr Slammer: business card
Rachel: jewellery, including earrings and necklace; purse on strings

SCENE 5

On stage: Bed
Harmonium
Pickwick's washing things including toothbrush

Off stage: Breakfast tray (**Mrs Bardell**)

SCENE 6

On stage: Braziers

Off stage: Pistol case (**Officer**)

Personal: **Winkle:** brandy
Dodson: writ

ACT II

SCENE 1

Off stage: Banners (**Crowd**)

SCENE 2

On stage: High stools and desks

SCENE 3

No props required

SCENE 4

Set: As Act I, Scene 2

LIGHTING PLOT

Only essential cues are given here. Further cues may be included at the Director's discretion.

ACT I, SCENE 1

To open: Exterior lighting.

Cue 1	As last of traders exits *Subdue lighting for scene change*	(Page 3)

ACT I, SCENE 2

Cue 2	**Chorus** (*singing*): " ... helps the poor debtors". (Fourth time) *Lights up on Scene 2*	(Page 3)
Cue 3	**Sam** " ... old *George and Vulture.*" *Lights down to low level with spot on Pickwick and Sam*	(Page 8)
Cue 4	**Pickwick** (*singing*): "That's where it all began." *Crossfade to* George and Vulture. *Night*	(Page 9)

ACT I, SCENE 3

Cue 5	**Chorus** (*singing*): "Merry Christmas." *Lights up on scene*	(Page 10)
Cue 6	Music for ballroom begins *Change lights to ballroom location*	(Page 20)

ACT I, SCENE 4

Cue 7	At end of Music 7 *Lights crossfade to Pickwick's bedroom*	(Page 26)

ACT I, SCENE 5

Cue 8	**Winkle** looks tragic *Crossfade to river, exterior lighting*	(Page 41)

ACT I, Scene 6

Cue 9   As **Pickwick** disappears beneath the ice   (Page 45)
         Black-out

ACT II, Scene 1

To open: General lighting

Cue 10   **Pickwick:** "Out of the way, man."   (Page 49)
         Concentrate lighting on hotel room

Cue 11   **Pickwick, Wardle** and **Rachel** leave inn   (Page 51)
         Increase lighting on square

Cue 12   On cue   (Page 53)
         Crossfade to office, keeping Pickwick in focus

ACT II, Scene 2

Cue 13   **Lawyers** (*singing*): "... three bishops and a
         whore!"   (Page 59)
         Begin crossfade to courtroom

ACT II, Scene 3

Cue 14   **Chorus** (*singing*): "Hear, hear, hear, hear." (Fourth
         time)   (Page 63)
         Begin crossfade to prison

ACT II, Scene 4

Cue 15   During Music 19   (Page 71)
         Crossfade to exterior lighting

ACT II, Scene 5

Cue 16   During Music 21   (Page 72)
         Lights up for Curtain Calls

EFFECTS PLOT

Only essential effects, as given in the script, are listed here.

ACT I

No cues

ACT II

Cue 1   At end of Coda to Music 18   (Page 69)
           Hunting horn

Typeset in Great Britain by Butler & Tanner Ltd, Frome and London

Downs Rd.

Hosp

Station